Closer Than My
Shadow

by

Diane Hanny

Illustrated by Richard Henkel

Logos International
Plainfield, New Jersey

CLOSER THAN MY SHADOW
Copyright ©1979 by Logos International
All rights reserved
Printed in the United States of America
Library of Congress Catalog Card Number: 78-71688
International Standard Book Number: 0-88270-350-1
Logos International, Plainfield, New Jersey 07060

*In memory of
my loving mother,
Ann Gruver*

Table of Contents

Foreword xi
Preface—Note to Parents xv

Part One: The Little Voice Inside
1. That Funny Feeling Inside 3
2. What Should I Do? 7
3. What Language Is That? 11

Part Two: The Gifts He Gives
4. Why Can't I Go? 21
5. How Did He Know That? 27
6. Poor, Poor Smokey...........................31
7. The Healing Touch 35
8. We Just Can't Get Out! 39
9. Why Is It So Quiet? 43
10. I Just Can't Sleep 47
11. That Strange Language......................51

Part Three: Caring and Sharing
12. Let's Have a Picnic! 59
13. Being Sick Is No Fun! 65
14. It's a Tornado!...............................69
15. Just Too Short! 73
16. We Didn't Mean to Do It 77

17. The Yellow Dress 81
18. All Those Years 87
19. "Hey, Freckles!" 91
20. I Just Love Horses 95

Part Four: A Wonderful Helper
21. A Wonderful Helper 105
22. Do You Believe in Electricity? 109
23. The Jesus Club 113
24. There Isn't Enough Food! 119
25. I Feel Better Now 123
26. Can I Help? 127
27. Let's Have a Walk-a-Thon 131
28. I Just Don't Understand 137
29. Now I Understand 141

Part Five: Walking With My Friend
30. Let's Pray About It 147
31. Does It Really Say That? 151
32. A Friend Named Jesus 157
33. Where Have You Been? 161
34. Oops! I Forgot! 165
35. I'm Gonna Punch You! 171
36. Jack Did It 177
37. He Loves Me No Matter What! 183
38. I Don't Need Your Help! 189
39. Don't You Ever Get Tired? 197
40. To Be a Winner 203

Foreword

On the Day of Pentecost, Peter quoted the prophet Joel:
"And in the last days it shall be, God declares, that I will pour out my Spirit upon all flesh, and your sons and your daughters shall prophesy, and your young men shall see visions, and your old men shall dream dreams; yea, and on my menservants and my maidservants in those days I will pour out my Spirit; and they shall prophesy."

(Acts 2:17-18 RSV)

When I read Diane Hanny's book, *Closer Than My Shadow*, I was excited to see she had caught a broad vision of the body of Christ. Yes, our children are members of the body of Christ just as much as the adults. I have seen churches where the children have been ignored concerning the functioning of the body of Christ and I have seen other churches where they have been recognized as members of the body. It never ceases to amaze me how God uses our children to bring home truths in such a manner that only a childlike faith can express. What a need there is for us to become like children in our walk of faith!

This present move of the Holy Spirit is not for this generation only. It must be passed on through teaching of the Word and by our example. What we have learned in our walk in the Spirit can be taught to our children and God will build upon that foundation. As I view the future I can see the absolute necessity for the believer to be filled with the Holy Spirit. The spiritual gifts will be indispensable tools for future conquest for Christ, making it possible for His Church to become that glorious Church without spot or wrinkle (Eph. 5:27) which Christ will present to himself.

Our children are vital keys to the future. They must be trained now! They must be equipped! I feel Diane's book is a timely instrument which will be used to awaken our children to the activity and power of the Holy Spirit. As I read her book I recognized the Holy Spirit's guidance to bring adult concepts of the Spirit to a child's level of understanding.

I have known Diane for many years. She was one of my Sunday school pupils and I have seen her grow in Christ through the years. Her ministry has been mainly to children and God has blessed that calling by an enthusiastic response from the children she has taught.

I know the Holy Spirit has truly inspired this book. Praise God for His precious Spirit working through the lives of yielded vessels! There is no limit to our ability when the Spirit makes us able!

I recommend *Closer Than My Shadow* to every parent. I suggest that parents and children read and discuss it together. It will be a tool for spiritual growth for all.

Robert Hahn, Elder
Fremont Christian Center
Fremont, Ohio

Preface

Note to Parents

The charismatic movement has swept across this country and the world in the past few years bringing thousands of people into a new realization of God, Jesus Christ and the Holy Spirit.

One group of people who desperately need to know what this all means is our children. Many youngsters sit through these meetings wide-eyed and frightened. This happens not because they don't like the service, but because they don't understand what is taking place.

If these children knew and understood the movings of the Holy Spirit, they would better be able to participate in and benefit from the services. This is why I felt the need for this book.

Closer Than My Shadow attempts to explain the gifts of the Spirit, the fruit of the Spirit, the ministries of the Spirit and some basic Christian principles for daily living.

Each subject is approached from a biblical point of view. The topics are applied to daily situations and taught on a level that can be understood by the very young.

This devotional is designed to reach children from four to ten years of age. With your help, the younger children can understand and relate to these stories. The older ones will enjoy reading and studying them on their own.

Scripture enforces each principle and you will find questions at the end of each lesson to insure proper understanding. This also allows for the interjection of thoughts you might have on any given subject. Each lesson is closed with a simple prayer.

I hope you find this book helpful in the spiritual growth of your children and in drawing your family together.

Special thanks to Robert and Gerry Hahn for their

prayerful assistance in the completion of this book and to Karen Sorg for typing the manuscript. Also many thanks to all those who prayed for and encouraged me throughout the writing process.

God bless you.

Diane Hanny

PART ONE

The Little Voice Inside

1
That Funny Feeling Inside

Terah and Teah were sisters; in fact they were twins. They lived in a pretty little house in the country with their parents.

Now Terah and Teah were twins, but that didn't mean they were always alike. They looked a lot alike, but they didn't think alike.

Terah liked flowers, pretty clothes, soft kittens, and Sunday school. Teah liked mud puddles, blue jeans, horses, and climbing trees.

Because Terah liked Sunday school so much, she had asked Jesus into her heart a long time ago and she loved Him more every day.

Teah was always in Sunday school, physically, but her thoughts were usually miles away. So Teah never heard much of the lesson or the sermon in church each Sunday.

One morning, about halfway through the sermon, Teah sat straight up in the pew. The preacher was talking about Jesus and how much He loved children. He told about how Jesus would talk with the children and how He healed them when they were sick. Teah thought this was quite unusual for any grown-up to do, so she listened a little harder.

The preacher continued, unaware of Teah's sudden interest. "Jesus loved us so much that He was willing to die for us. He died to pay for our sins. We all have sinned, even if we don't think we have. Romans 3:23 says, 'For all have sinned, and come short of the glory of God.' We are born in sin, so even if we can't remember one bad thing we have ever done, we still are sinners."

He continued, "We have to ask Jesus to forgive us for being sinners. We have to ask Him to come in and cleanse our hearts."

When Teah heard that, she had a funny feeling inside. She reached over and grabbed Terah's arm. "Hey, what's he talking about? I just had a funny feeling inside, like I should do what the preacher just said."

Terah looked a little surprised. "Well, that's the Holy Spirit telling you that you still have sin in your heart that Jesus needs to take care of. All you have to do is pray and tell Jesus you are sorry for the naughty things you've done and ask Him to come into your heart and cleanse it. Then just believe and trust Him to do it."

Teah had to think that over for a while, but when the preacher asked if anyone wanted to receive Jesus that morning, she went forward and asked Him to come into her heart.

SALVATION

Scripture reading: John 16:7-8

This Scripture tells us it is the Holy Spirit who shows us we are sinners. To be a sinner does not mean we are mean and wicked people. Sin does not have to be something terrible; it can be as simple as eating three cookies when mother told you to take only two.

Sin can also be something we *don't* do. For example, if your mother tells you to put the papers in the garbage can outside and you just dump them in the kitchen wastebasket, and go to play, that is a sin. Not because you dumped the papers in the trash can, but because you didn't do the whole job. That is a form of disobedience.

It is wonderful that God is so loving and forgiving. Even if we make the same mistake over and over, He still loves us and forgives us. All we have to do is ask Him. Just tell God you are sorry for doing wrong and ask for His forgiveness through His Son, Jesus. This is one prayer God will always answer.

Questions:
1. Who told Teah that she still had sin in her heart?
2. Have you ever felt that feeling inside like Teah did?
3. What should you do about that feeling?
4. Would you like to invite Jesus into your heart right now?

Prayer:
Dear Jesus, I know I have sin in my heart. I am sorry for all the bad things I have done. I want you to come into my heart and forgive me right now. In your name, amen.

2
What Should I Do?

One day when Laura and her younger brother, Mike, were on their way to school, Mike found something in a pile of leaves on the sidewalk.

"Hey, Laura, look what I found! It's a billfold, and look at all this money. Wow!"

"Is there a name in it?" Laura questioned. "Maybe we can find the person who lost it."

"I'm not sure I want to find them. There's seven dollars here. We could buy a lot of candy and other goodies with that much money," Mike answered.

"I still think we should try to find the owner. Let me see it," Laura insisted.

As she looked through all the pockets in the billfold, she found a paper that had the name of Alvin Grant on it. "I wonder if this is the guy who lost it. There isn't an address, so we'll have to look in the phone book after school."

"Now wait just a minute, Laura. I'm the one who found the billfold and I didn't say I wanted to return it."

Laura looked stunned. "Don't you remember what the Bible says about stealing?"

"Yeah," Mike said. "But I didn't steal this; I just found it."

"Okay then, I guess it's your problem, I'm going to school." With that, Laura walked on, leaving Mike standing there with the billfold in his hand.

After school Mike was still carrying the billfold around and trying to figure out just what was the right thing to do. Something kept telling him to call Mr. Grant to let him know about the whole thing. Was it really stealing to keep it?

Laura didn't say much all the way home that night, but Mike knew what she was thinking.

When they got home, Mike got the phone book and started looking through it. When he found the right number, he slowly dialed.

"Hello, Mr. Grant?" Mike asked.

"Yes, who is this?" questioned the stranger.

Mike hesitated, "I—I'm Mike Bradner. Did you lose your billfold?"

"Why, yes, I did. Did you find it?" the man asked.

"I sure did," Mike said, "and I thought you might want it back, so I called."

"Thank you so much for being an honest young man. I'll come right over and pick it up."

Mike told Mr. Grant where he lived and soon he was coming up the front steps. Mike was a little nervous when he opened the door.

"Hi. Well, here it is, and all the money is still there."

"Well, thanks again for being so honest and here is a little something for a reward." Mr. Grant pulled out a dollar bill and handed it to Mike.

"Wow, thanks a million!" said Mike.

Mike didn't have seven dollars to spend, but at least he could really enjoy spending the one he did have, and Laura was very happy with the decision Mike had made.

GUIDANCE

Scripture reading: Proverbs 3:5-6

According to God's Word, we are to trust totally in the Lord for our guidance. We are not to lean on our own understanding but we are to trust in Him.

If we tell God all our plans and problems, He will show us where to go and what to do. When we pray about something, God's Holy Spirit guides us and helps us make the right decision.

We can tell it's the leading of the Holy Spirit by the peace and joy we feel when we choose the right way.

Questions:
1. Why did Mike want to keep the billfold?
2. Would it be the same as stealing if he had kept it?
3. What was it that kept telling Mike to call Mr. Grant?
4. Do you think Mike did the right thing?

Prayer:
Dear Lord, help us to always call on you when we need to make decisions. Show us how to hear and know your voice, and to be obedient. In Jesus' name, amen.

3
What Language Is That?

"Come on, Chris, or we'll be late for church," mother said as she tapped on the bathroom door.

"Okay, I'll be right out. Just one more flip of the comb," Chris answered.

All the way to church Chris sang songs of praise to the Lord. He had so much for which to be thankful. Just this past week God had done several wonderful things for him.

On Monday the Lord helped him find dad's car

keys. Wednesday night at church the Lord healed him of a sore throat. On Friday, God had made a way for him to go to the stock car races, and Saturday he received his acceptance forms for church camp in the mail. What a fantastic week!

As the church service began, Chris found that he really wanted to tell God how thankful he was for all these blessings. He started praying and praising the Lord. Before long Chris was saying things he just couldn't understand. The more he praised the Lord, the more these strange sounds came pouring out of his mouth. He felt so warm and joyful inside, that he knew it was a special visitation of the Holy Spirit.

After church, Chris asked his mother and dad about what had happened. They told him he had experienced what is known as the baptism in the Holy Spirit and that the strange words he had spoken were his new prayer language—a language for him to use whenever he wanted to talk to the Lord and didn't know what to say, or when his heart was so full of love and joy that he just couldn't find words to express himself.

Chris had found a new depth in his walk with the Lord and also learned that he had a new power to witness and to serve the Lord better every day.

THE BAPTISM IN THE HOLY SPIRIT

Scripture reading: Acts 2:2-4

Jesus promised to send a Comforter to His disciples after He went back to heaven. The Holy Spirit is that Comforter.

We receive the Holy Spirit into our lives when we invite Jesus into our hearts. Soon the Lord becomes more important to us than anything else. More important than our family, our friends, our home, money or even that new bicycle or doll you got for your birthday.

Finally, we reach a place where we want to be yielded completely to God. We want to serve Him with the same power Jesus had. This is when we ask for the baptism in the Holy Spirit.

We can receive this in many ways. No certain way will be right for everyone. No two people are alike, and God works with each one of us in His perfect way.

Very often people receive the baptism in the Holy Spirit when they are praising the Lord. When we can no longer find the right words to tell Jesus how much we love Him, the Holy Spirit gives us words in a heavenly language we cannot understand. This is called "speaking in tongues."

This is not the same as the gift of tongues we will study later. This heavenly language is used in our private prayer time when we are alone with God, or in our praise to God during a service when the whole group is praising the Lord. We might also use this prayer language when we are praying for someone or something and we don't know just what to pray for. We don't always need to understand what we are saying because God understands all our prayer languages.

It might help us to understand this if we think of a cup of water. When we receive Jesus as our Savior, our cup is half full. When we make Jesus the Lord of our lives, our cup is full to the brim. When we receive the baptism in the Holy Spirit, our cup overflows with the joy of the Lord. When our cup overflows, we often need this prayer language to express our happiness and to tell Jesus how much we love Him.

With this new joy also comes new power. It is the same power Jesus had and used to heal the sick and perform miracles.

These three steps in our spiritual lives can take either a few minutes or several years; it all depends on you.

Questions:
1. Can everyone have a prayer language?
2. Do we always understand our prayer language?
3. Have you ever spoken in a prayer language?
4. How full is your cup?

Prayer:
Dear Lord, help us to understand these things about your Holy Spirit. Show us how full our cup is and how full you want it to be and show us how to serve you better each day. In Jesus' name, amen.

PART TWO

The Gifts He Gives

Now there are diversities of gifts, but the same Spirit. (1 Cor. 12:4)

For to one is given by the Spirit the word of wisdom; to another the word of knowledge by the same Spirit; To another faith by the same Spirit; to another the gifts of healing by the same Spirit; To another the working of miracles; to another prophecy; to another discerning of spirits; to another divers kinds of tongues; to another the interpretation of tongues. (1 Cor. 12:8-10)

4
Why Can't I Go?

Karl just couldn't understand why his dad wouldn't let him go to summer camp. He knew it wasn't because of the money; he had planned to pay for it with his allowance. He had been saving for several months just so he could go.

As he sat looking out the window and thinking about his problem, his dad came in the front door.

"Karl, would you take out the garbage?" he asked.

"Why should I take out the garbage? I never get to

do the things I want to do, like going to summer camp. I'm not taking out that smelly old junk; let Johnny do it when he gets home from his paper route."

"Karl, this is your responsibility so I expect you to do it."

Karl knew his dad meant business so he did empty the garbage, but he was grumbling all the way and he didn't do a very good job of it, either. Karl figured if he didn't do a good job, the next time dad would ask Johnny to do it. Johnny always did a good job.

Later that evening when mother came home from the grocery store, Karl and his dad had another argument.

"Karl, would you please help me carry in these grocery sacks?" dad asked.

"Dad, I'm busy. This is my favorite TV show and it is almost over. Just wait a few minutes."

"But, Karl, I need your help now!"

"Oh, all right, but just wait, I'll get even for making me miss the end of that show. After all, I have some rights around this place."

With that, Karl stormed out the back door and nearly pushed his mother off the porch on the way.

That evening Karl and Johnny were looking at the papers about summer camp and Johnny was filling out his application.

"Dad, why can't I go to camp this year?" Karl asked. "I have more than enough money in the bank and all I need is for you to sign the permission slip. Please."

"Karl, we have been through this all before. I am going to need your help with important projects this summer. Perhaps you can go to camp next year. Now I think it would be best if you would go on to bed."

Karl was furious, but he knew better than to say any more when his dad used that tone of voice, so he went to bed.

The next day was Sunday so Karl talked with his Sunday school teacher about the problem. He explained just how important it was for him to go to summer camp, especially since Johnny was going.

Mr. Evans thought about it for a few minutes and prayed silently before he tried to answer Karl.

"Karl, let's talk about God for a minute."

"Well, I don't see what He has to do with summer camp, but if you think it will help, okay," Karl said.

"God loves each one of us very much, Karl. He also wants to give us the desires of our hearts. But we need to learn that we also have something to give. We need to give God our love, respect, and obedience. This isn't always easy, but God still expects it of us. It isn't enough just to be obedient; we need to show our respect and love for God by joyful obedience and true respect for Him. If God knows that our hearts are right and that we do love and respect Him, then He will want to give us the things we want."

"So what does that have to do with summer camp?" Karl asked.

"You think about it, Karl. If you were God and someone was always disobedient and cocky with you, would you give him special gifts?"

"Of course not. I wouldn't give him anything, except maybe a good punch," Karl answered.

"Then look at your dad's position. I have seen you be very disrespectful to him, even at church. I have seen you disobey and rebel against him. I have watched your cocky attitudes. What would you do if you were your dad?"

Karl didn't answer Mr. Evans; he just ran out of the room. He tried to forget what he had heard, but deep inside Karl knew it was true. Karl didn't deserve to go to camp.

If Mr. Evans had just started to scold Karl for his wrongdoing, Karl would have walked out and thought his dad had already talked with his teacher. God gave Mr. Evans the wisdom to show Karl what the real problem was. Karl had to decide what his next move would be.

WORD OF WISDOM

Scripture reading: 2 Samuel 12:1-7a

David had committed a sin against God. God sent Nathan, a man who walked close with God, to talk to David about what he had done. Nathan knew that if he made King David mad at him, he might be killed and then God's message would not be delivered.

God helped Nathan to understand how to deal with David. Nathan told him a story about another man and it made David very mad at the man in the story. He knew this man had done a terrible thing in the sight of God and man. Then Nathan told David that the man in the story was David himself. The king was very upset by this, but he knew Nathan had brought the word from the Lord. David was sorry for doing wrong and asked God to forgive him.

This is an example of how God gives his people the gift of wisdom. Wisdom is knowing the right thing to do, the right thing to say at the right time and place.

Questions:
1. Why didn't Nathan just tell David he had sinned?
2. Why couldn't Karl go to summer camp?
3. How did Nathan and Mr. Evans know what to say?

4. Do we need to know the right thing to say?

Prayer:
Dear God, help us to seek your wisdom before we try to solve a problem. Show us where the trouble is and what we should do about it. Give us your wisdom so we can do what is right in your sight. Thank you, Jesus. Amen.

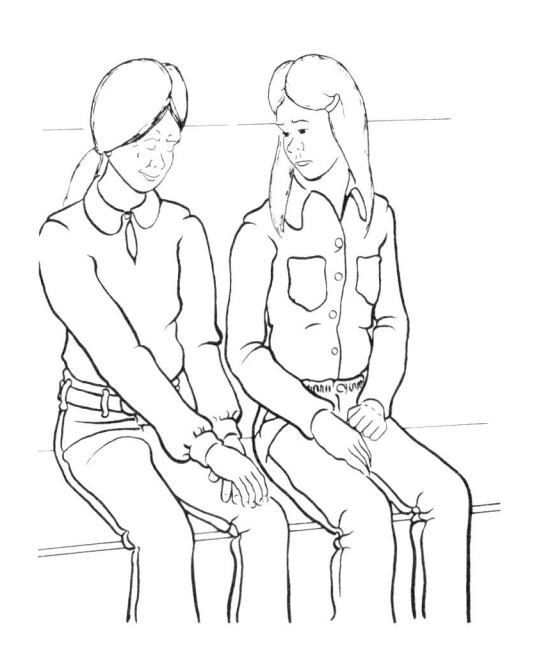

5
How Did He Know That?

One time Lisa went to church with her friend, Nancy, to hear a missionary speaker. The service was beautiful and the music was something special. Lisa and Nancy were both really enjoying the service.

Suddenly Lisa started feeling sharp pains in her legs. This had never happened to her before so she was a little scared, but she didn't say anything to anyone.

At the close of the service the speaker interrupted his prayer. "Someone in the group is having severe pains in her legs and if she will come forward for prayer, the Lord will heal her."

Lisa almost jumped out of the chair. She grabbed Nancy's arm. "How did he know that? I didn't even tell you about my legs hurting."

God had given the speaker the gift of knowledge to reveal the problem with Lisa's legs. When she went up for prayer, the Lord healed her. God received glory not only for the gift of knowledge, but also for the healing, and Lisa went home with a new friend named Jesus in her life.

WORD OF KNOWLEDGE

Scripture reading: John 4:28-29

This story tells us of a woman Jesus met at Jacob's well one day. He was thirsty and asked her to draw some water from the well for Him. As she did this, Jesus began speaking to her about the things of God and the promise of the kingdom to come.

While they talked, Jesus told her of all the bad things she had done in the past and how she would have to change if she wanted to enter into the kingdom of God.

Jesus had never met this woman before, yet God showed Him these things about her that no one else knew. God did this to prove to the woman that Jesus was the Christ, the Savior of the world.

God used this special gift of knowledge to bring glory to His name and to bring this woman to salvation.

This is not a gift that only Jesus had. Every person who has the Holy Spirit within them can have this same gift, whenever God sees that they need it.

Questions:
1. What gift was Jesus using when He talked to the woman by the well?
2. Was the gift just for Jesus?
3. What made Lisa almost jump out of her chair?
4. Who gets the glory for this gift?

Prayer:
Dear Lord, help us to trust you in all things and show us how to use this gift of knowledge. Help us to understand the workings of your Holy Spirit so that our lives can bring glory to your name. Amen.

6
Poor, Poor Smokey

"Mom! Come quick! Smokey is real sick," Jimmy said.

"Okay, I'll be right out," mom answered.

Putting down the dish towel, mom went out to look at Smokey. Smokey was the family pet, a big gray cat. He was lying in the wagon in the garage.

"Oh, my, he really is sick. You better not play with Smokey until daddy gets to look at him," mom cautioned.

"But, mom, he looks so lonely, and when I'm sick I want someone to love me. Can't I just sit with him?" Jimmy begged.

"Well, okay, but don't touch him."

Before long dad came home from work. He and mom had a talk about Smokey and decided that things didn't look very good. In fact they felt that Smokey would probably be dead by the next morning.

"Jimmy," dad began, "I don't think Smokey is going to get well, so I want you to be ready for it if it happens. But if he does die, we can get you another kitten."

"I don't want another cat—I love Smokey. Can't we pray for him?" Jimmy asked.

"I guess we can," mom said. "I don't know if God will heal Smokey or not, but it can't hurt to ask."

So the three of them prayed and asked God to take care of Smokey. Mom and dad weren't so sure God would answer a prayer about a cat, but Jimmy never doubted it for a minute.

"I just know God is going to make Smokey be all better real soon," Jimmy told his mother. "I just feel something inside of me that says God will answer our prayer."

"I hope you're right, Jimmy," mom said.

The next day Jimmy couldn't wait to get outside to check on Smokey. When he found him, he was still lying in the wagon. Jimmy's heart nearly stopped beating as he walked over to touch Smokey. When he put his hand on Smokey's head, the cat looked up and purred softly.

"Mom! Mom! Smokey is better," Jimmy cried. "Look, his eyes aren't runny any more and he's hungry. Thank you, God, for making Smokey get better."

"I'm so glad God loves us enough to even make our pets feel better," mom said. "But I know it was your faith that made it all happen. Dad and I weren't sure about it, but you never doubted for a minute and God honored your faith in Him."

GIFT OF FAITH

Scripture reading: Matthew 14:28-30

This Scripture explains the gift of faith. This helps us understand a little better just how it works. Peter knew that by all natural standards it would be impossible for him to walk out on the water without sinking. God gave Peter the gift of supernatural faith that made it possible for him to really walk on the water.

Peter believed Jesus would not have told him to

come out on the water unless He knew it was possible. So Peter, trusting in the faith God gave him, started walking on the water towards Jesus. Everything went just fine until Peter started thinking about the waves splashing around his feet. Then he took his eyes off Jesus. When he lost sight of Jesus, he forgot to trust his God-given faith.

If Peter had kept his eyes and mind set on Jesus, he would have completed his walk on the sea, and his faith would have brought him through to safety.

The same is true in our lives today. Sometimes God gives us a strong faith to believe in something that seems impossible. We know in the natural that it can never happen, yet if we trust God to do the work, He always comes through.

Questions:
1. What did Peter do by faith?
2. Can we have this kind of faith today?
3. Do you remember ever having this kind of faith in your life?
4. Why did Smokey get better?

Prayer:
Dear Lord, help us to remember that you are still as powerful as you were in Peter's day. Teach us how to trust in you alone and give us this gift of faith the next time we find ourselves in an impossible situation. In Jesus' name, amen.

7
The Healing Touch

"Let's play tag," Joey said.

"Okay, you're it," Karen yelled as she took off across the meadow.

They were running and laughing and having lots of fun. Suddenly Karen screamed and fell to the ground. "I twisted my ankle. I tripped in that hole over there."

"Are you all right?" Joey asked.

"No. I don't think I can walk," Karen moaned.

By now Karen was in tears and Joey wasn't very happy either. Karen cried because her ankle hurt and Joey worried because he was scared and didn't know what to do. Then he remembered something they had learned in Sunday school that week.

"Karen, the Bible says that if we ask for healing in the name of Jesus and believe He will do it, He will. We better pray and ask Jesus to heal your ankle," Joey said. "Otherwise, we may not get home before dark. You sure can't walk on it the way it is."

"No, I can't walk on it now; it hurts too bad. And we're too far from home to call for help, so let's pray."

So Karen and Joey prayed for the sore and swollen ankle to be healed. They trusted Jesus to do the healing, and when Joey put his hand on Karen's ankle, all the pain left.

"Wow!" Karen said. "That was really neat. It doesn't hurt any more. Thanks, Joey."

"Praise the Lord—not me," Joey said.

So Karen and Joey got up and walked back home. They got back long before dark and they had much to tell their parents and much for which to praise the Lord.

GIFT OF HEALING

Scripture reading: Acts 3:2, 6-8

Peter and John had gone to the temple to pray and teach. As they entered the temple, they saw a handicapped man begging for money.

They didn't have any money to give the lame man, but they knew Jesus had the power to heal, if they would ask Him.

As Peter prayed, the lame man also believed in Jesus and he was healed.

Then the man went walking and leaping through the Temple and he praised God for this wonderful gift of healing.

Questions:
1. Who healed Karen's swollen ankle?
2. Where did Joey learn about healing power?
3. In whose name did they pray?
4. Can you also receive healing through this gift?

Prayer:
Dear Lord, let us always remember that you love us and want us to walk in perfect health. Teach us to trust in your name for our healing. In Jesus' name, amen.

8
We Just Can't Get Out!

Ken and Toby had been playing outside very peacefully for quite some time. Then suddenly mother heard them yelling and crying. She ran out the back door and found they had locked themselves in the garage.

"Mom! Help us! We can't get the door open," Toby cried. "We wanted to play in here for a while, so we locked the door to keep Julie out."

"I've tried to open it from in here and the handle

just won't move," Ken said.

"Okay, boys," mother began. "Just calm down a little and try the handle again."

Ken pushed and pulled on the door, but it just wouldn't budge. By this time Toby was getting really scared and Julie was standing outside the garage in tears.

"Julie, you stay here and talk to your brothers," mother said. "I'm going to get the key ring."

Soon mother returned with a long chain of keys. She put each key in the lock and tried to turn them. There was one that fit, but there was no handle on the outside of the door. Dad had warned the boys not to lock the garage door because of the broken handle. Now they knew why.

"Boys, there just is no way to unlock that door, except if you do it from inside," mother concluded. "The windows are too small for you to crawl through and there is no handle out here to turn."

"But I can't move the handle in here," Ken insisted. "It just won't move."

"I think we'd better pray and ask God to handle this mess," mother said. "Otherwise you may be in there all night."

So Julie and mother prayed on the outside and Toby and Ken prayed on the inside. Then they continued trying to open the door. Toby was crying, Julie was screaming, mother was praying, and Ken was worried.

Then suddenly he calmed down. "Mom, I think I can open it now," Ken said.

With that, he reached up and turned the handle that released the lock.

"It wasn't even hard that time. I just barely touched it and it moved," Ken said, rather surprised. "Praise the Lord! It is a miracle I could move that old handle."

Everyone was very happy that the garage door was open now and they all thanked God for the miracle they had seen that afternoon.

GIFT OF MIRACLES

Scripture reading: Matthew 15:34-38

Jesus and His disciples only had seven loaves of bread and a few little fishes. This was hardly enough to feed twenty hungry people. Jesus asked God to bless the food and He performed a miracle.

Over five thousand people were fed that afternoon and when the disciples collected the leftovers, they picked up seven baskets full. That was a real miracle; they had more left over than they had to start with.

A miracle can be many different things. A miracle

is anything God can do that is impossible for us to do. It is anything God does that cannot be explained by natural means.

God does perform miracles today. He uses the gift of miracles to do this.

Questions:
1. Did Jesus' disciples go to the store for more food to feed the five thousand?
2. Where did the food come from?
3. Does God still perform miracles today?
4. What kind of miracle did Toby and Ken see?

Prayer:
Dear Jesus, help us to believe that miracles can still happen today. Show us when we need to ask for a miracle and help us to trust you to do the work. Amen.

9
Why Is It So Quiet?

One morning during the church service everyone suddenly became very quiet. It was so still that Lisa could hear herself breathing. Then a man in the back of the building started to speak.

He told of how much God loved us and how happy He was when we praised Him. Then the man told how the Lord wanted each one of them to study more and pray every day and that if they would do this He would bless their church. God promised that if the people were faithful in prayer and Bible study soon there would be so many young people that they would have to sit on the floor until a larger building could be found.

Lisa didn't quite understand all this, but the older people seemed to be very happy about what the man said. He had given a special message—called a prophecy—that is another gift of the Holy Spirit.

Many months passed and it seemed that everyone had forgotten what occurred that morning. Lisa knew the people had been growing closer to the Lord because she could see it in their lives by how they loved one another.

What the man had said on that Sunday morning began to happen. Soon the young people started coming in. At first it was only one or two at a time. Then they started a Bible study for college-age people and soon the prophecy was fulfilled. The young people were sitting all over the floors and the leaders of the church were looking for a bigger place to hold their meetings.

GIFT OF PROPHECY

Scripture reading: Luke 1:41-45

God showed Elizabeth that the baby growing inside her cousin, Mary, was going to be our Lord and

Savior. No one could have even known if it would be a boy or a girl, unless God told them.

Even after Jesus was born, few knew He was the Son of God. Yet, Elizabeth knew long before His birth that Jesus was the promised Savior. This is an example of the gift of prophecy.

Prophecy can either tell of something that will happen in the future, as with Elizabeth, or it can come as a message for someone right at the moment.

Many prophecies today are words of comfort or encouragement, or they just tell us of God's wonderful love. So prophecy doesn't have to tell some future event; it can just be a special message of love and encouragement.

Questions:
1. How did Elizabeth know about the baby Mary was going to have?
2. Does prophecy always tell of the future?
3. What else can prophecy tell?
4. Have you ever heard a prophecy?

Prayer:
Dear Lord, show us when the gift of prophecy is being used and help us to understand what you are telling us. If you ever want us to bring a word of prophecy, help us to be obedient. In Jesus' name, amen.

10
I Just Can't Sleep

Todd had a problem. He just couldn't seem to go to sleep at night. Ever since he and Billy had gone to see that monster movie last month, Todd couldn't sleep well. He really wasn't afraid of the dark; he just didn't want to close his eyes. Every time he closed his eyes, he could see, hear, and almost feel those ugly monsters all around him.

Todd and Billy had talked about it and the same thing was going on in Billy's life. The boys tried to pray about it and they tried to convince themselves they really weren't scared of anything, but it just didn't help.

Finally Todd told his parents about the problem. They knew at once that these fears were not from God. Todd and Billy had become afraid because of looking at the monster movie. This kind of movie is not pleasing to God and can cause problems.

After Todd's parents prayed for them and asked Jesus to take away the problem, their fears were gone. Todd and Billy could then get a good night's sleep.

God had given these parents the gift of discernment so they could get rid of the fears and the boys could once again sleep peacefully. Todd and Billy also learned the importance of not watching and listening to things that are not pleasing to God.

DISCERNMENT OF SPIRITS

Scripture reading: Acts 13:6-12

We see here that Paul is talking to the governor about the Lord Jesus. Elymas was trying to convince the governor that this story of Jesus being the Savior was not true. God gave Paul the gift of discernment so he knew how to deal with Elymas. God revealed that the problem was an evil spirit rather than just a doubtful man.

To understand this gift of the Holy Spirit, we must first understand that there are two forces at work in the world today. There is a good force, which consists of God, Jesus Christ, the Holy Spirit and the ministering angels. The bad force is the devil and his demons. The gift of discernment is when God shows us which force is at work in a certain situation.

Questions:
1. Why couldn't Todd sleep?
2. Where did Todd and Billy get these fears?
3. How did Todd's parents know what the problem was?
4. Have you ever really been afraid of something?

Prayer:
Dear Lord, help us not to do or see things that will let fears get into our lives. Show us when evil is near and help us to remember that in your name we can chase the fears away. Jesus, be our friend. Amen.

11
That Strange Language

Dodi and Jeff never paid much attention to what was going on during church services. They thought they were too little to understand it anyway. One morning the singing was especially beautiful, so they were listening intently.

Suddenly everyone became real quiet. Then Mr. Keith stood up and started to speak. But what in the world was he saying?

"Dodi, what is he saying?" Jeff asked.

"Good grief, Jeff, I don't know. Just listen and see what happens."

Mr. Keith continued the message for several minutes, then he sat down.

After a few minutes passed, Mrs. Duken stood up and began to speak out in English. God was telling the people of His love for them and of the things He would do if they would obey His Word and draw close to Him.

Everyone in the service was happy and excited by what God told them. They all went home with new joy and strength in their lives. God uses tongues and interpretation to encourage His people. In this way God can speak to a whole body of believers.

The gifts of tongues and interpretation are separate, but they must always be used together. If one brings a message in tongues and there is no interpretation, something is wrong. Either the message in tongues is not from God, or someone is not obedient about bringing the interpretation.

GIFTS OF TONGUES AND INTERPRETATION

Scripture reading: 1 Corinthians 14:5-6

Paul explains that if you use the gift of tongues in

the church, someone will be given the understanding of what you say.

In a service when you hear many people praying and singing in tongues all together, this is the prayer language they received when they experienced the baptism in the Holy Spirit. This is not the same as the gift of tongues with interpretation.

When the gift of tongues is used, usually the service becomes very quiet and then one person speaks out loud and clear in tongues (a language you can't understand). Then there is usually a pause and someone will repeat the message in English, so that everyone in the service can understand what God is saying. Sometimes the same person has both the tongues and the interpretation.

Questions:
1. What are tongues?
2. Can you tell the difference between the gift of tongues and your prayer language?
3. What other gift must be used with tongues?
4. Does the gift of tongues ever work alone? Why not?

Prayer:
Dear God, help us to understand this lesson on the gift of tongues. Show us when this gift is in our services. Teach us to use it in our own lives and not be afraid to speak it forth. In Jesus' name, amen.

PART THREE

Caring and Sharing

But the fruit of the Spirit is love, joy, peace, longsuffering, gentleness, goodness, faith, meekness, temperance, against such there is no law. (Gal. 5:22-23)

12
Let's Have a Picnic!

It was a beautiful spring day and Patty just couldn't wait to get outside. She was going to ask her mother if they could all go on a picnic after church. She and her brother, Bobby, could feed the ducks at the park and then play on the swings.

As Patty finished brushing her hair, she ran to the kitchen to talk to her mother.

"Mom, can we go for a picnic today after church? It is so nice out and Bobby and I could feed the ducks. It would be such great fun. Please."

"That does sound like fun, Patty, but aren't you forgetting something?" mother asked.

"Forgetting what? I don't remember anything that I had planned for today."

"Oops," Bobby chimed in, "we promised to visit Mrs. Dobson this afternoon. She gets so lonely now that her son moved away."

"Oh, Bobby, we can visit her any day, but it is just perfect for a picnic today," Patty insisted.

Mother gave Patty a thoughtful look. "Patty, sometimes it is more important to keep our promises than it is to do our own thing. We all love picnics, but I think Mrs. Dobson would be very disappointed if you didn't visit her today."

"Yeah, I guess you're right, mom. We can have our picnic some other day," Patty agreed.

Bobby went out in the garden and picked some pretty spring flowers to take to Mrs. Dobson. "I think these might cheer her up," he said. "Don't you, mom?"

"Yes, Bobby, that's a lovely idea. Now you two better scoot or she'll think you've forgotten her for sure."

Patty was glad she had decided to keep her promise to Mrs. Dobson and was feeling quite happy by the time they rang the doorbell.

"Well, look who is here!" Mrs. Dobson exclaimed.

"Do come in, children, and see what I have made for you."

A big pitcher of milk and a plate of their very favorite chocolate chip cookies had been placed on the table. "I have been baking all morning," she said. "Now come and let's chat while we have our cookies. Then you may take the rest home."

Bobby, Patty and Mrs. Dobson talked for a long while that afternoon and Patty really did enjoy herself. She hadn't realized how much their visits meant to Mrs. Dobson. Now she was glad they hadn't gone on the picnic.

When they got up to leave, Patty could see tears in Mrs. Dobson's eyes. "Don't cry, Mrs. Dobson. Maybe next week we can go on a picnic and you can come, too. Wouldn't that be nice?" Patty asked.

"Oh, that would be just peachy," she said, "and I can bake some more chocolate chip cookies for the picnic."

"That's a super idea, Mrs. Dobson," Bobby said.

With that they all said good-bye.

FRUIT OF LOVE

Scripture reading: Matthew 22:37-39

These are the words of Jesus. He tells us we are to

love the Lord God with all our heart, soul and mind. Then we are to love our neighbor as ourselves. This doesn't mean just the people who live next door or down the street from us. Jesus is telling us to love everyone as much as we love ourselves.

We all like to do what *we* want to do. We like to have the biggest piece of cake or the most peanuts at the ball game. This is just the way people are naturally. When we ask Jesus into our hearts, this should change. Jesus always put the needs of others before what He wanted to do. Many times Jesus would go without food and rest just to teach and heal the people who were following Him. Jesus is our example and we should try every day to grow more like Him. This is how people who don't know Jesus will know we are Christians. "By this shall all men know that ye are my disciples, if ye have love one to another" (John 13:35).

Questions:
1. How can people tell if we really love Jesus?
2. Who was the first one to show love toward Mrs. Dobson?
3. How did Mrs. Dobson show her love for the children?
4. How did Patty feel when they left Mrs. Dobson's house?

Prayer:
Dear Lord, help us to love you more than anything else. Show us ways to be more loving toward others. Jesus, we love you and want to grow more like you every day. Amen.

13
Being Sick Is No Fun!

Susan was a very sick little girl. She had to stay in bed for several weeks to get her strength back. Many of her friends came over to cheer her up, but they soon discovered they were the ones who were being cheered up—by Susan.

Susan didn't like being in bed and missing school. She really wasn't excited about staying in the house and watching her friends through the window. But she was happy in her heart because she knew Jesus was her Savior and that soon she could run and play again. The joy of the Lord gave Susan the strength to be patient until she was completely well.

Neal was also very sick, but he was very unhappy. When his friends came to visit, he was so grumpy that they never stayed long. Then Neal began to get mad at God. He thought God was being mean by letting him be sick. Soon Neal decided he didn't need Jesus as his friend any more, so he suffered through his sickness alone.

Both Susan and Neal recovered from their sicknesses, but with very different results. Susan had gained many new friends and had brought several people to Jesus because of her joyful attitude.

Neal had lost most of his buddies from school because he was so nasty to them when they would visit. He also blamed God for his sickness, so he no longer felt God's love.

FRUIT OF JOY

Scripture reading: Romans 15:13

We can have joy in our lives at all times if we are serving God. This means that even in a time of trouble and sickness we can have joy in our hearts, because we know our hope is in Jesus and He never fails.

We not only *can* have this joy, we *should* have it. If we have the Holy Spirit within us, we should show forth this fruit of the Spirit.

No one likes someone who goes through life with a frown on his face. Christians need to be especially careful that they don't act like Mr. Gloom-and-doom. Smiles are contagious, but to keep a smile on our faces we need joy in our hearts.

If you read through some of Paul's letters in the New Testament, you will find that he understood what it meant to have joy during trials.

He and his friends were very often in hard places. Once when Paul and Barnabas were in jail, the guard found them singing. They had been laughed at, beaten up and thrown into a cold, dark prison. Does that sound like something to be happy about?

Paul wasn't happy because he was suffering, but he was joyful because he knew he was where God wanted him to be and he was doing what God had told him to do. He had placed his complete trust in God and His Son, Jesus. That is why Paul was joyfully praising God even in a very bad situation.

Paul also wrote many encouraging letters to the early churches while he was in prison. He had learned that no matter what kind of mess he found himself in, he still had the joy of the Lord for his strength.

We need to understand that just because we don't get exactly what we want or because we are going through a hard place, is no reason to lose our joy. If we lose our joy in the Lord, we may lose the very strength we need to get through the problem.

Questions:
1. Was Paul glad that he was in prison?
2. Where did Susan get her joy?
3. Why was Neal unhappy?
4. What good came from Susan's joy?

Prayer:
Dear heavenly Father, sometimes we feel so sad and don't want to praise you. When things go wrong, it is hard to be joyful. Help us to trust you even when things look bad. Show us how to let the joy of the Lord be our strength. In Jesus' name, amen.

14
It's a Tornado!

Matt and Marti were out playing in a summer rain with their friend, Denny. Suddenly the wind began to blow very hard and lightning flashed across the sky. The children all ran to the front porch to watch the storm in safety.

"Boy, that sure came up fast," Matt said.

"Yeah, we better go inside so we don't get hurt," Denny replied, pointing nervously to the front door.

"It's safe right here, Denny. Jesus will take care of

us," said Marti.

Just then the wind blew very hard and a tree fell across the street.

"I'm getting out of here!" yelled Denny, and he ran inside.

Matt and Marti followed him. When they got inside all the lights were out. The wind had torn down the power lines so there was no electricity in the house.

"You children stay inside," mother said. "The news said there is a tornado coming our way."

"A tornado!" Denny cried. "I want to go home. I'm scared. What if it hits your house?"

Mother took Denny by the hand and Matt and Marti joined her in prayer. "Dear Lord, keep us safe from this storm and help Denny not to be afraid. Show us your peace. Amen."

After a moment of quietness she said, "God has this storm under control so we don't have to worry. Let's all just stay close together. When the lights come back on we can have some cookies," mother said.

Denny wasn't so sure anyone could control a storm like that, but Matt and Marti just started playing as if nothing was going on outside.

When the storm was over, Denny went back home, but he was determined to find out just who was controlling that storm.

FRUIT OF PEACE

Scripture reading: John 14:27

Peace is the opposite of worry, upset and strife. According to this Scripture, Jesus left His peace with us when He returned to heaven. Jesus never worried about anything because He knew He was doing His Father's work and God would provide for all His needs.

If we have Jesus in our hearts, we are also God's children and this enables us to have peace in our lives, too.

Peace is like the joy we just studied in that we don't have to depend on good circumstances for it to show forth in our lives. We can have God's peace regardless of what is going on around us.

Questions:
1. Why was Denny scared?
2. What did mother do?
3. Who gives us peace?
4. When should we worry and be afraid?

Prayer:
Dear Lord, help us to know your peace. With the world upset like it is, it is easy to become worried and

afraid. Give us your peace so that others may want it, too. In Jesus' name, amen.

15
Just Too Short!

Greg grumbled as he went upstairs with his arms full of folded clothes. "I sure wish Debbie would learn to put her own things away!"

Debbie was his little sister and she just wasn't quite tall enough to reach all of her dresser drawers, so Greg had the job of putting her clean clothes away every wash day.

On this particular day Greg was especially upset because he had to leave a baseball game to do the job.

"Mom, I really think Debbie could do this by herself. I get so tired of doing her work. I have more important things to do with my time," Greg argued.

Mother smiled and said, "But, Greg, you need to be patient with your sister. After all, she is only four years old and when you were four, you didn't put your clothes away either. When Debbie gets a little taller, she will put her own things away."

"But, mom," Greg protested, "it's such a bother to drop what I'm doing to do her work. It just doesn't seem fair."

"Greg, do you remember last summer when you needed help to learn to ride your bicycle?" mother asked.

"Yeah, so what?"

"Well, Ted had to drop his work many times to help you with that bicycle. Sometimes he was right in the middle of a project with his friends, but he stopped to help you because he is your brother and he loves you. He learned to be patient with you, and soon you no longer needed his help. That's how you need to treat Debbie," mother said.

Greg thought about it for a minute. "I guess you're right; after all, she can't stay short forever," he said. "And we would get along better around here if I didn't grumble about it so much."

Mother agreed and gave him a big hug.

FRUIT OF LONGSUFFERING

Scripture reading: Psalm 37:7

This Scripture tells us to be patient. We should not become anxious about anything, but are to trust in God for everything. We can't look at all the nice things the unbelievers have and become jealous, because they may have done evil to get them. We are to be patient and keep a pure heart before the Lord, and in His time He will bless us with even more than we ask.

We also need to learn to be patient with each other. We don't like people to lose their patience with us, so we can't lose patience with them.

When we ask God to increase our patience, we'd better get ready for some trials and temptations. In James 1:2-3 it tells us: "My brethren, count it all joy when ye fall into divers temptations; knowing this, that the trying of your faith worketh patience."

So we see that to allow the fruit of longsuffering or patience to grow in us we need to work hard at overcoming the trials and temptations that come our way.

We also need to remember how patient God is with us. If God gave up and got mad at us every time we made a mistake or were disobedient, we would always be in trouble. God is very loving and longsuffering toward us and if we are His children, then we will learn to show forth the same kind of attitudes toward others that our heavenly Father shows toward us.

Questions:
1. Why do we need to learn patience?
2. Is God patient with us? How?
3. Why did Greg get so mad at Debbie?
4. How do we learn patience?

Prayer:
Dear God, help us to show forth patience in our lives. Teach us how to love others and to be slow to anger. Show us how to let this fruit grow in our own lives. In Jesus' name, amen.

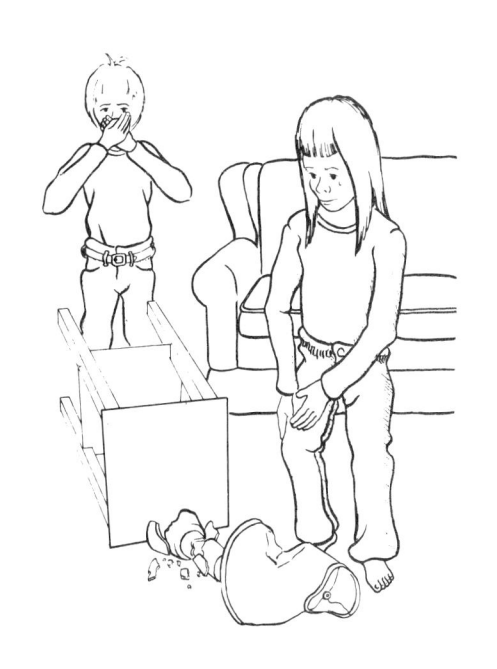

16
We Didn't Mean to Do It

Mother stood in front of the kitchen window drying the supper dishes. She could hear Sherri and Keith in the other room.

"You kids better settle down in there before you break something," she called.

"Okay, mom, we will," Keith answered.

Before long mother heard a loud crash and then someone crying. "What in the world happened?" she asked as she ran to the front room.

She found Sherri sitting on the floor with an antique lamp smashed at her feet. She was crying and there was blood trickling down her hand.

"I'm so sorry, mom. I tried to clean it up, but look what happened," Sherri whispered.

"We were playing tag and Sherri ran into the end table," Keith explained.

"Didn't I just tell you two to stop playing so rough in the house?" mother asked. "Now come on and let's take a look at that cut."

Mother gently led Sherri to the bathroom. She could see how sorry and afraid both children were, so she didn't scold them. After mother washed and bandaged Sherri's hand, she finished cleaning up the broken glass.

Even though mother had not become angry with Sherri and Keith, they had been disobedient; so when dad came in from the garage that evening, they had a little family talk.

"I realize this thing with the lamp was an accident," dad began. "But you both knew better than to play tag indoors, so you will have to be punished."

At this point Keith began to grumble and Sherri began to cry. Mother felt a little sorry for Sherri; she had already learned her lesson because of getting cut, but mother also knew it wouldn't be fair to punish only Keith.

"I think you both should go straight to bed tonight," dad began, "and no television for a week. I know breaking the lamp was an accident, but you both need to learn to be obedient to your mother and me. Now go on and get ready for bed."

With that Keith and Sherri scooted off to bed. Their parents had handled the problem with authority, but they lessened the blow with love and gentleness.

FRUIT OF GENTLENESS

Scripture reading: Titus 3:2-5

Paul told the early Christians to be gentle and speak evil about no man. We must remember that we also make mistakes and do wrong things. If we expect others to be kind and understanding of our mistakes, then we must also be gentle with them when they do things we don't like or say things that hurt us. Jesus is our example in displaying all the fruit of the Spirit. He was gentle with all men.

The dictionary says that gentleness is a quality to be formed in people of noble birth. It means we should be polite and courteous. Even when we use our spiritual authority, we can still be gentle if we do it in love. Since we are of the family of God, this fruit should be growing in our lives also.

Questions:
1. What fruit of the Spirit are we talking about in this lesson?
2. Why do we need to be gentle?
3. Why did Keith and Sherri get punished?
4. Do you think Jesus would have handled the problem in a different way?

Prayer:
Dear Lord, teach us how to love those who hurt us. Bless us with the fruit of gentleness. Show us how to be like Jesus in all ways. Amen.

17
The Yellow Dress

Christy was so excited when she ran through the front door after school. "Hey, mom, there's a new girl in my class. Her name is Liz and I just know we are going to be great friends!"

"That sounds real nice, Christy. Does she live near here? Maybe she could come over to play some night after school," mother said.

"Gee, I don't know. I'll ask her tomorrow at school."

Christy and Liz liked each other right from the start. They enjoyed the same kind of games, liked the same boys and just seemed to be two of a kind.

After several weeks had passed, Christy began to wonder why Liz always wore the same two dresses to school.

"Liz, why don't you wear some of your other clothes to school? Don't you get tired of those two dresses?"

Liz looked like she was going to cry. She had hoped no one would notice she only had two dresses. "I can't wear what I don't have," she said. "I only have those and my dad has been out of work for a long time because of a car accident. We are all so glad that dad wasn't killed, that we don't mind not having a lot of clothes."

Christy was sorry she had asked. When she got home from school that night, she began looking through her closet. As she counted her dresses, she was almost ashamed because she had so many.

"Mom, do you think Liz would like some of my dresses?" Christy asked. "She is a little smaller that I am so I could give her some that are getting too short for me."

"That's a fine idea. Have her come over after school tomorrow and try them on. Then she can take whichever ones she likes," mother suggested.

Liz was so excited about getting some new

dresses, that she could hardly wait to try them on. After she had picked out several outfits, Liz noticed a pretty yellow dress in the back of the closet. "Can I try that one on?" she asked.

Christy gulped as she handed her the dress. That one was her favorite. It was a birthday present from her grandma. It was a beautiful dress with white lace trim and a ruffled skirt. Mother had even bought her a bright yellow hat to go with it for church.

"Oh, my!" Liz exclaimed, as she paraded in front of the mirror. "It's just beautiful."

"My grandma got it for my birthday," Christy said. "I only wear it for church. Here, try on the hat too."

After admiring herself in the mirror for a few minutes, Liz put the yellow dress back on the hanger and hung it in its special corner of the closet. She knew how Christy felt about that dress and was very content just to have been allowed to try it on.

"I'll pack all these things in a box for you and you can get them after school Friday," mother said.

"That will be great," Liz answered. "I can hardly wait to show mom and dad."

That night after supper Christy went upstairs to help her mother pack up Liz's things. She took her yellow dress from its hanger and sat on the bed gently stroking the ruffled hemline. "Mom, could I give this dress to Liz, too?" she asked.

Mother was a little surprised. "But Christy, that is

your very best dress, and I thought it was your favorite."

"Well, it is, but Liz looks so pretty in it and I know she loves it just as much as I do. I really think she needs it more than I do. She'll be so happy if I give it to her."

Mother gave Christy a little hug. "Sure. You can give it to her if it is that important to you."

When Friday night came Liz was beside herself. She was so thrilled about the new dresses that she almost didn't notice the bright yellow dress hanging on the closet door.

Christy took the dress off the door and handed it to Liz. "I want you to have this one, too. It looks so nice on you, that I think you should have it."

When mother walked past the door she saw Liz and Christy hugging and laughing and crying all at the same time. It was then that she knew for sure Christy had made the right decision in giving Liz the yellow dress.

FRUIT OF GOODNESS

Scripture reading: Galatians 6:9

Goodness can be shown in many ways, but each way should tell people we love the Lord Jesus. In

Matthew 5:14-15 we are told to be the lights of the world. Through our good works people can see Jesus in our lives.

Goodness is a fruit that must be put into action. It is not enough that we have good thoughts about someone or have a good idea of how to help a friend. If we don't put our thoughts into action, that friend will never know we want to help him.

Jesus was always looking for ways to help people. He helped through sharing food with those who followed Him. He also helped by healing the sick and teaching people how to be good disciples. Jesus taught that Christians should help the poor and needy. He taught that we are to put others' needs before our own. That means if your friend is hungry and you only have one sandwhich, you should be willing to share your food so that you both can have something to eat—even if you are hungry enough to eat three sandwiches all by yourself.

Questions:
1. How did Jesus show goodness in His life?
2. Why did Liz need clothes?
3. Was it her fault that she only had two dresses?
4. What did Christy do that made her gift so special?

Prayer:
Dear Jesus, help us to grow more like you every day. Show us ways to put our good thoughts into action. Teach us to be lights in our neighborhood. In your name we pray, amen.

18
All Those Years

Mrs. Adams had been teaching Sunday school for twenty years. She had been Mr. Kent's teacher when he was a child and now she was teaching his son, Paul.

Mrs. Adams was there almost every Sunday for her class. The only times she missed were when she was sick or on vacation. The children loved her because she was always smiling and made her lessons so interesting.

Besides teaching, Mrs. Adams always helped with the Sunday school parties and the summer picnics.

One day Paul asked her a rather odd question. "Mrs. Adams, don't you ever get tired of teaching Sunday school?"

"Well, Paul, we all get tired from time to time, but that is no reason to quit. As long as the Lord needs and wants me to teach, I'll be available," she answered.

"I sure wouldn't want to do the same thing every week. Don't you ever feel like staying home and resting?" Paul asked.

"Yes, sometimes I feel like throwing that alarm clock across the room and burying my head in the pillows, but that isn't what God expects of me. He has put me in a position of responsibility and He expects me to be faithful to Him."

Paul just shook his head. "Sure seems like a lot of work," he said.

"It is," she agreed, "but Jesus put in a lot of work for our benefit and I am sure He got very tired at times. Still, Jesus stayed here and was faithful until He finished the work He had been called to do. If Jesus is faithful to us, we should also be faithful to Him."

"I guess you're right. I just haven't known Jesus long enough to trust Him the way you do. I hope someday I will be as faithful to Him as you are, Mrs.

Adams," Paul continued.

"I know you'll be faithful in your calling too, Paul. It just takes time to learn to lean completely on Jesus and always let Him control your life."

Paul chuckled, "Well, at least I found out why you are still teaching Sunday school, and now I have some other things to think about too."

FRUIT OF FAITH

Scripture reading: 1 Corinthians 4:2

We must first understand that faith as a gift of the Holy Spirit is not the same as faith as a fruit of the Holy Spirit. We learned several lessons ago about the gift of faith, which is a special faith that is given by God in certain situations.

The fruit of faith is something that must grow just like fruit grows on a tree. It takes a long time to grow fruit, but only seconds to receive a gift.

To grow this fruit of faith we must learn from experience that God is always faithful in what He says. God never fails to keep a promise and He never tells us something that isn't true. As we begin to put our complete trust in Him, we should become as faithful to Him as He is to us. We should also be faithful to others.

When we tell someone we will do something or be somewhere, we should be sure we keep our word. To an unbeliever this can be either a good testimony for Jesus or a bad one. If we begin breaking our promises and fail to do what we say, soon people will no longer be able to trust us.

If we want others to have faith in us and in our God, we need to be faithful to them and to the Lord. In this way people will know we have complete trust or faith in God.

Questions:
1. How do faith and faithfulness work together?
2. Which comes first—faith in God or faithfulness to Him?
3. How was Mrs. Adams faithful to the Lord?
4. Do you think Paul was drawn closer to the Lord through what Mrs. Adams said?

Prayer:
Heavenly Father, help us to put our complete faith in you. Then show us where we are to be faithful in your service. Let us draw others to you by our fruit of faithfulness. In Jesus' name, amen.

19
"Hey, Freckles!"

George was usually a very happy young man, but on this particular evening he was a little down in the dumps.

"What seems to be the problem, George?" mother asked.

"Oh, the kids at school started calling me 'Orangey' today. They think my red hair is something to laugh about."

"Well, at least they quit calling you 'Freckles,' " mother said with a twinkle in her eye.

"Yeah, I guess that is one good thing about it. I just wish they wouldn't call me anything except George."

The next day at school, George dreaded time for recess. He knew the kids would be calling him names again. He sat at his desk remembering how the people mocked Jesus and called Him names. They even hit and spit on Jesus. No one had done anything that bad to George. He decided he should try to act like Jesus did and not get upset with his school friends.

Just then, George's thoughts were interrupted by the recess bell. He whispered a little prayer as he put on his jacket.

"Look, here comes Orangey. He looks like he ran into a paint brush," Randy laughed.

"Yeah, I bet his mother tried her new hair dye on him to see what color she would get!" Mike yelled.

George could feel his face getting red as he listened to the boys making fun of his hair. He felt like punching them right in the nose, but he also knew that wasn't the right thing to do.

"Hey, Freckle-Face, why is your face getting red?" Marvin asked. "Did you swallow a match? Your head's on fire!"

"You guys are all wrong," George said. "The reason my hair is red is because God knew that green hair wouldn't match my freckles. And all those freckles are just marks from where the angels were kissing me."

They all started to laugh. "Come on, let's play ball," Marvin said. "George, since the angels like you so well, you better be on my team. We need all the help we can get."

"Okay, let's go," answered George.

George had not only prevented a big argument and maybe a fist fight, but he also left the boys wondering just what made him act the way he did. Did God really have anything to do with it? Did George really have angels watching over him? What if God heard us call him Orangey? These were some of the questions the boys asked George in the weeks to follow. This gave George many chances to witness for the Lord.

FRUIT OF MEEKNESS

Scripture reading: Matthew 27:13-15

In this Scripture we see a perfect example of meekness. Of course, we know Jesus is our perfect example for everything.

Even when men took Jesus into court and accused Him of many bad things, He still didn't try to defend himself. Jesus stood silently before the judge and knew His Father was in control of even that. If Jesus had been anything but meek, He would not only have answered the accusations, He probably would have become very angry about them.

Jesus has given us an example of how to be meek. It is our job to put this into action in our own lives.

Questions:
1. Why was George upset when he came home from school?
2. What did Jesus do when people called Him names?
3. What fruit did George show to his school friends?
4. What do you do when your friends tease you?

Prayer:
Dear Lord, because we love you so much, we want to be like you in every way. Meekness is hard for us to show to others. Please help us to remember your example and pattern our lives after you. Thank you, Jesus. Amen.

20
I Just Love Horses

Brenda just loved horses. Every night after school she and her friend, Pam, would walk over to Mr. Arden's farm and watch the horses. Before long, they began riding them. Hours would pass and the girls wouldn't head for home until it started getting dark. When they did get home, they usually were too tired to do their chores.

"Boy, I'm going to take a shower and go to bed when I get home," Pam moaned.

"That sounds like a great idea," Brenda agreed.

The only problem was that Brenda had work to do when she got home. Each one in her family had jobs to do and no one else would do her jobs unless Brenda was sick. She was tired, but she certainly wasn't sick.

"Mom, why didn't Luke finish the dishes for me? After all, I was busy this afternoon and now I still have homework to do," Brenda grumbled.

"Luke did his chores," mother answered. "The dishes are your responsibility. And you should have done that homework before you left for Mr. Arden's place."

"Why do I always have to do the dishes? Can't someone else do them for a change?" Brenda argued. "You and dad do whatever you want to. No one tells you where to go or what to do."

"Now just a minute, young lady!" dad interrupted. "We get our work done first and no one needs to keep reminding us. Sure we do a lot of fun things, but only after we finish our chores. You want to ride horses all day and then come to a hot meal and a soft bed, with no work on your part. I'm sorry, but it just doesn't work that way—not at our house."

About that time, Luke walked in. "Dad, can I go to the park after school tomorrow with John?" he asked. "I took out the trash tonight and I can finish painting the fence in the morning before school."

"Sure, Luke, you go ahead. Just be home in time

for supper," dad answered.

"See what I mean," Brenda started. "Luke gets to do everything he wants and I can't even go riding without getting yelled at."

"Brenda, that's enough!" dad said with a very stern look on his face. "When you learn to use a little self-control you will be treated that way too. From now on, you do not go to Mr. Arden's or anywhere until your homework and housework are done. Do you understand?"

"Yeah, I understand," Brenda mumbled. She knew better than to argue any more. When dad got that look on his face, it was time to keep quiet.

You must understand that there wasn't anything wrong with Brenda's love for horses. The problem started when she let them become the most important thing in her life. When we let anything except God's Holy Spirit rule our lives, we are not practicing temperance.

FRUIT OF TEMPERANCE

Scripture reading: Philippians 4:5

The word "moderation" is used in this Scripture,

but it means nearly the same thing as temperance. Temperance simply means we practice self-control. This means in all areas in our lives—eating, talking, temper, sports, or anything else that is important to us.

Sometimes it is hard to practice self-control, like when there is a whole plate of cookies on the table and you know dinner will be ready soon. Even if mother doesn't tell you how many to eat, you know two is enough. Temperance is to keep your hand from reaching for the third or fourth cookie.

This, like many of the fruit of the Holy Spirit, takes time and effort to grow. Self-control is hard because our bodies or minds tell us one thing and our spirits tell us something different. Like on Sunday morning when your body says, "Stay in bed and sleep" and your spirit says, "Get up for Sunday school." Temperance is when you allow the spirit to win over the flesh.

Questions:
1. Why didn't Brenda do her work before she rode the horses?
2. Did Luke practice self-control?
3. Was Brenda's dad wrong in correcting her?
4. Where do you need to use self-control in your life?

Prayer:
Heavenly Father, help us today to practice self-control in all things. This is very hard for us because it is so much easier to let the flesh control. Teach us to draw on your strength to bring forth this fruit in our lives. In Jesus' name, amen.

PART FOUR

A Wonderful Helper

And there are differences of administrations, but the same Lord. (1 Cor. 12:5)

And God hath set some in the church, first apostles, secondarily prophets, thirdly teachers, after that miracles, then gifts of healings, helps, governments, diversities of tongues. (1 Cor. 12:28)

21
A Wonderful Helper

God had begun a new church body in the village of Cherry Grove. The people were excited about all the wonderful things God was showing them.

However, they soon started to have some problems in the church. The men began to argue over certain teachings and Christian principles. They realized they needed some direction from God, so they met together and prayed that He would send someone to teach them the correct rules they should follow.

At the same time a brother in a nearby city had felt the Lord leading him toward the Cherry Grove fellowship. Mr. Shux had long since been recognized as an apostle by his own church and had ministered to many new churches in this way. As he earnestly prayed, he felt he should go to speak with the elders of the Cherry Grove fellowship.

After the meeting, it was decided that Mr. Shux would minister and teach at Cherry Grove at least once a week until the Lord directed otherwise.

Mr. Shux started with the very basic Christian beliefs. He helped them to sort out right doctrines and lay aside those which were wrong. He taught the people how to respect each other's differences of opinion, instead of using them to build walls between themselves.

Along with his teaching, Mr. Shux also counseled the people who were having personal problems in their Christian walk. He worked together with the eldership of Cherry Grove. He also encouraged many new ministries in that body of believers.

God sent Mr. Shux to get this new church established. It wasn't that the elders didn't know what they were doing, but rather that they needed their energies to be channeled in the right directions. When people are beginning a New Testament church, they sometimes get confused. When they stress one gift or one ministry too much, they often forget about the others. An apostle will show them how to correct these problems and how to use all the gifts and ministries of the Holy Spirit.

Because of the great responsibilities he has, we can see that a man called to be an apostle must be a mature Christian.

MINISTRY OF AN APOSTLE

Scripture reading: 2 Peter 3:2, Acts 5:12

An apostle is a messenger or leader who is sent by God to help a certain group of believers. His job varies with the needs of each group he is called to serve.

An apostle preaches the Word of God. He helps churches get established and become grounded in the truths of God. He will correct them if they have had wrong teaching.

An apostle is also a counselor to the church. He will help smooth out rough spots. He gives guidance through the wisdom of God.

God often uses an apostle to encourage brothers and sisters who are just stepping out in their ministries in the church. He teaches them how to follow God's directions.

Of course, most apostles also have all the gifts of the Holy Spirit operating in their lives, which helps them greatly in this ministry.

Questions:
1. Why did Mr. Shux go to Cherry Grove?
2. Why couldn't the elders take care of the problem?
3. What does an apostle do?
4. Have you ever been under the ministry of an apostle?

Prayer:
Dear God, help us understand just what an apostle is. Show us how this ministry can benefit each believer and how we can help this ministry in our own church. In Jesus' name, amen.

22
Do You Believe in Electricity?

Mrs. Higgins had planned a lovely picnic for her Sunday school class. While they sat on the blanket eating their lunch, the children began to ask questions.

"How do you know God is really there?" Betty asked, pointing to the sky. "I can't see Him and I can't hear Him."

"Yeah, and how do you know Jesus ever really rose from the dead?" Paul challenged. "I know none of us were there when it happened."

Mrs. Higgins smiled at the children. "Sometimes it is hard for us to believe in things we can't see or touch," she began. "We can believe in the sun and the moon because we can see them, and we can feel the warmth of the sun on a day like today. It isn't quite so easy with spiritual things."

"I'll buy that," said Peter. "But I know God is real; I can feel Him inside of me. The problem is trying to explain that to someone who has never known Jesus."

All the children chimed in, agreeing with Peter.

"Do you all believe in electricity?" Mrs. Higgins asked.

"Sure we do," they all responded.

"Well, have you ever seen electricity? We see lights, and machines running and maybe some sparks flying when a line is down, but that isn't really the electricity. These are evidences that the electricity does exist, but it isn't really the power itself," she explained. "That's how it is with God. We can see He is real through nature, the laws of the universe, healings, and miracles that happen every day, but no man has ever seen the fullness of God."

"I never thought of it that way," said Peter. "It's just like the air we breathe; you can't always see it, but it is there just the same."

"That's right, Peter. We don't have to see and feel

something to believe in it. That is where faith comes in. We believe in Jesus because the Bible tells us He is the Son of God. We have never seen Him, but by faith we accept Him."

Mrs. Higgins continued, "The Bible tells us—'Jesus saith unto him, Thomas, because thou hast seen me, thou hast believed: blessed are they that have not seen, and yet have believed' (John 20:29). That is us."

"Gee thanks, Mrs. Higgins. Now I have an answer for people when they question my faith in God," Peter said.

"You're very welcome, Peter," she replied.

You see, Mrs. Higgins didn't intend to teach during their picnic outing, but when God wants a lesson taught, He doesn't always do it in a church building. All He needs is a willing and capable teacher and people who want to be taught.

MINISTRY OF TEACHERS

Scripture reading: Matthew 28:19-20

This is Christ's Great Commission to us to go and teach others about Him. This doesn't mean we only teach within the church walls. We are to go out into the world around us and tell others about Jesus and His wonderful love.

The teaching ministry in the local assembly of believers doesn't mean teaching only in church or Sunday school. Of course, that is part of it, but we also can teach people in our homes, on the street corner or walking down the sidewalk.

The dictionary says that to teach is to show someone how to do something, to give instructions or to train. We can even do this while talking over a glass of Coke or while eating pizza.

Questions:
1. Where does God use His teaching ministry?
2. Was Mrs. Higgins working within this ministry?
3. What did she teach the children?
4. Did you learn anything from her lesson?

Prayer:
Dear Father, help us to understand about the ministries of the Holy Spirit. Show us when you want us to step into a ministry. Give us the faith to trust you when we cannot trust ourselves. In Jesus' name, amen.

23
The Jesus Club

Tina and Greg had talked many times about starting a Jesus Club for the kids in their neighborhood, but now it seemed even more important. Every time Tina prayed, she felt it was time to get the club started, but she just wasn't sure it was God's voice she was hearing.

One day on the way home from school, Tina decided to ask Greg about it.

"Greg, have you thought any more about the Jesus

Club?" she asked.

"Yeah, Tina, in fact that is all I have thought about for the past two weeks. It's almost like the Lord is saying that *now* is the right time."

"Have you talked to your parents about it?" Tina asked.

"No, I haven't mentioned it to anyone, except you. I want to be sure this is what the Lord wants before I say anything or start making plans," Greg said.

"Well, I have been praying about it, too, and it just seems that the time is right to start it now," Tina agreed.

"I think you're right, Tina, but I want one more nudge from the Lord, and this time from someone we don't know," Greg said.

One night the following week Tina and Greg went to a special service at a friend's church. The speaker was from Oklahoma and had never met them, so he couldn't have known about their plans for a Jesus Club. His name was Clark Garry.

During the song and praise service, Mr. Garry called Greg and Tina to the front. "I have a word for you from the Lord," he said.

"The Lord said He has shown you two something to do and now is the time to begin. Everything will fall into place and there will be no problems He will not take care of. Many children will benefit from your club ministry and will come to know Jesus. The Lord will truly bless both of you and you will see others blessed also. Even this week a place will be provided for you to work in, so go and be about His business."

Tina and Greg were so excited that they could hardly sit through the rest of the service. Everything they had prayed about was mentioned in the prophecy, and they knew Mr. Garry had no way of knowing about the Jesus Club unless God had told him.

The following Tuesday after school, Mr. Raber, the neighbor down the street, came down to talk to Greg. "Greg, do you know anyone who could use my old shed? You know, for storage or something. I just don't need all that room any more," he said.

Greg nearly shouted. The Lord had provided a place for the club to meet. When Greg told Mr. Raber what they were doing, he gave them an old rug and several chairs to use. Their parents thought it was such a great idea that they furnished a table and lamp and the mothers took turns baking cookies for the meetings.

Before long the Jesus Club was in full swing and many children had been drawn closer to the Lord through its ministry. Everything Mr. Garry had said came to pass and many people, both young and old, benefited from the Jesus Club.

MINISTRY OF A PROPHET

Scripture reading: Acts 11:27-28

A prophet is an appointed messenger of God. His ministry varies from church to church and from meeting to meeting. He speaks forth the word of God. He has God-given understanding; by the Holy Spirit he can foretell things that will happen. He also gives direction in the ministry, worship and doctrine of a church. All these responsibilities of a prophet are directly inspired by the Holy Spirit. No man could know and do these things without God's help.

In today's Scripture the prophet Agabus foretells a great famine. A famine is a time when there is little or no food. This Scripture also states that the prophecy was fulfilled in the days of Claudius Caesar.

We must first understand that one way of knowing whether a prophet is sent from God is that his prophecies come true. We can also judge a prophecy by the Word of God, the Bible. God will not send a spoken message that goes against His written Word.

Another way to judge a prophet is by the fruit of the Holy Spirit. These are: love, joy, peace, longsuffering, gentleness, goodness, faith, meekness, and temperance, which we studied in the last section of this book. If a man is a true prophet of God, these fruits should be seen in his life.

So we see that there are at least three tests of a prophet of God: 1. Does his message line up with the written Word of God? 2. Does his message come true at some time in the future? 3. Does his life show forth the fruit of the Holy Spirit?

If a person does not pass these three tests, he is not a true prophet of God, and we should not receive his messages as from God.

Sometimes a prophet speaks to a whole church body and sometimes he speaks to just one person. When he speaks to one person, it is called personal prophecy. This is usually just a confirmation of something God had already spoken to that person. When a prophet of God brings a word of confirmation to a person, it usually is a great encouragement for that person to continue in what the Lord has told him to do.

Questions:
1. Is everyone who brings a prophecy a prophet of God?
2. What are the tests of a true prophet?
3. Did Mr. Garry's prophecy come true?
4. Have you ever met a prophet of God?

Prayer:

Dear Lord, help us understand and benefit from all the ministries in your body. Give us your mind and wisdom to deal with each new lesson we are taught. And never let us put our trust in the person who brings the message, but only in God who sends the message. In Jesus' name we pray, amen.

24
There Isn't Enough Food!

Mother was busy baking cookies when Eddie came in. "Are those for tonight?" he asked. "I sure hope we have lots of food. I'm always starved after church."

"Yes, these are for the fellowship after church, but you needn't make a pig of yourself tonight," mother warned.

Eddie was very excited about the singers who were coming to church that night. He had heard them before and knew how good they were. Everyone was to bring something for a snack after church in the fellowship hall.

That night at church Eddie helped his mother and dad set up the tables and make the coffee. Several ladies brought back plates of cookies and snacks. Soon the sanctuary began to fill up, but the cookies stopped coming in. Mother began to get concerned. "Where are the rest of the ladies with their snacks?" she wondered. "I do hope there are more coming."

By the time the service began, there were nine plates of snacks on the table, but there were nearly two hundred people in the sanctuary listening to the music.

"What are we going to do about more food?" mother asked. "There isn't half enough to feed all those people. We don't even have time to run to the store for some chips."

"I think we had better pray," Eddie said. "If Jesus could multiply the fish and bread, He can multiply the cookies, too."

"I guess you're right," mother agreed. "Let's pray. We certainly can't let our guests go home hungry."

After they prayed, Eddie looked back at the table. "It still looks the same to me," he said. "I hope the Lord isn't finished yet."

Soon the people were filing through the refreshment line. Everyone took several cookies. Even Eddie had three.

"I don't believe this," mother said. "I mean I do believe it, but I never saw anything like this before."

"Yeah, isn't it neat?" Eddie said. "Can I have another cookie? There are plenty left and the adults are all finished."

"Sure, that will make less leftovers," mother chuckled.

When everyone was finished and the clean-up crew started, there were still some cookies left. God had performed a miracle by increasing the food. Everyone had plenty to eat and they even had some left.

"I sure am glad we asked God to multiply this food," Eddie said. "Now I even have some cookies for tomorrow."

MINISTRY OF MIRACLES

Scripture reading: Acts 6:8

The ministry of miracles is simply the gift of miracles within the local body. Of course, the gift of miracles can also happen outside the local body, because God causes this gift to be in action whenever and wherever it is needed.

In our Scripture for today, we see that Stephen

was full of the Holy Spirit and performing many miracles. In the very next chapter Stephen is stoned to death because of his deep faith in Jesus. This should tell us there is a price to pay, if we want to live for God and minister His gifts.

Some people believe the time for miracles is past, and that God no longer performs them today. I have seen too many miracles in my own life to think this way. God will always be in the miracle business because He is the same yesterday, today, and forever.

Questions:
1. What was the miracle in the story today?
2. Why did Eddie need a miracle?
3. Who brought the extra snacks?
4. Can God perform a miracle in your life?

Prayer:
Dear Lord, help us to believe in miracles even when others say it is impossible. Show us the miracles you put in our lives every day and let us praise you for them. In Jesus' name, amen.

25
I Feel Better Now

It was a beautiful Sunday and it seemed that almost everyone was at church. Gail and Becky were sitting in the back row giggling and passing notes back and forth.

Suddenly Becky started to cry.

"What in the world is wrong with you?" Gail asked.

"I don't know; I just got an awful pain in my stomach. It really hurts bad," Becky said.

"What should we do? Do you want the elders to

pray for you?"

"I don't know," Becky began. "What will they do to me?"

"Oh, Becky, they aren't going to hurt you. The men will just lay hands on you and pray. Maybe they will anoint you with oil, too," Gail answered.

"Well, I won't feel any better just because a bunch of people put their hands on me or put a little oil on my forehead. I may not be very smart, but I know that it takes more than that to get rid of all this pain. Oh, it hurts so much," Becky moaned.

Mr. Albert was leading the song service, so Gail tried to get his attention. First, she waved her hand at him, but he was lost in a song. Then she tried clearing her throat rather loudly, but no one noticed her. Finally, she stood up and waited until Mr. Albert saw her.

"What is it, Gail?" he asked. "Do you have something to share this morning?"

"Not exactly; I want prayer for my friend, Becky. She isn't feeling very well today," Gail replied.

"Well, Becky, come on up front here so we can minister to you," Mr. Albert said.

Becky was frightened, but she was so sick that she was willing to try anything. "Gail, come with me," she begged.

Taking Becky by the hand, Gail said, "I guess it will be okay for me to come up and pray with them."

Mr. Albert and several others laid hands on Becky and prayed for the pain to leave her stomach. They anointed her forehead with oil and then asked Gail to put her hand on Becky's stomach right where the pain was.

"Gail, what are you doing?" Becky asked, a little panic-stricken. "I can feel something warm going through my stomach, and the pain is gone. What did you do to me?"

Gail started to laugh, "I didn't do anything to you. Praise the Lord! You have just been healed by the power of the Holy Spirit. Isn't it neat?"

Becky didn't know if she thought it was neat or not. This healing stuff was just too new for her. "Well, I sure am glad you came with me. It was from your hand that I felt the warmth going into my stomach and as the warmth went in, the pain left."

"Well, I was just doing what the Lord told me to do. I was only the instrument God used this morning to bring healing to you. The glory goes to God," Gail answered.

MINISTRY OF HEALING

Scripture reading: Acts 3:2-8

Peter and John were going to the temple to teach

when they saw the lame man begging at the gate. They didn't have any money to give him, but they knew that through the name of Jesus they had the power to give him healing. Any person with the Spirit of God living in them has this same power. God doesn't only give it to one or two people; we all can have this gift if the situation requires it. We must remember, however, that God is the power source, and we are only His instruments.

Many times during a church meeting, someone will need a healing touch from Jesus. If you ever find yourself in a service and not feeling well or experiencing pain, don't sit through the service and go home sick. Ask someone to pray for you. God will give someone the gift of healing to minister to you.

Questions:
1. Has God ever used you in the healing ministry?
2. Have you ever been healed in a service?
3. Why was Becky scared at first?
4. Who really did the healing?

Prayer:
Precious Father, help us to understand the ministry of divine healing. Show us how and when to minister to others. Keep us pure so we can be used when we are needed. In Jesus' name, amen.

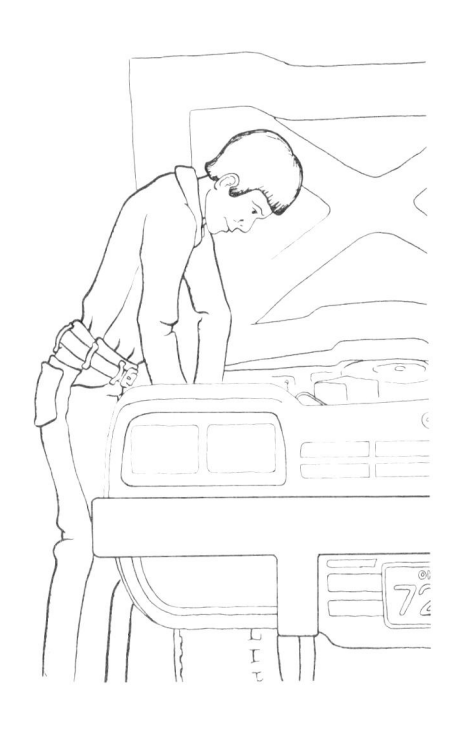

26
Can I Help?

Jim always thought he was the least of all when it came to the things of God. He didn't play a musical instrument, he couldn't sing very well, and he was afraid to speak in the service so he never brought a prophecy or did much sharing. Jim really felt like the Lord was keeping him on the shelf for some reason.

One afternoon a brother in the Lord called Jim on the phone. "Hey, Jim, can you come and help me work on my car tonight? I just can't figure out why it won't start," Dan said.

"Sure," Jim responded, "I'll be over right after supper."

After a few minutes they found the problem and corrected it. Soon Jim was back home and busy working on something else.

No one ever thought much about this being a ministry for Jim, but many people called on him for help with their cars.

Jim also was kept busy at church. They worshiped in a small building with a limited number of chairs. Whenever they had a large crowd, someone had to carry all the chairs from the classrooms to the sanctuary and then back to the rooms after the opening service. Jim always did this job.

It wasn't that someone asked him. He just saw that it needed to be done, so he did it. He also would make sure the heat was turned on during the winter months and that the air conditioners were working in the summer. Of course, others also helped with these jobs, but Jim was usually the first on the scene and the last to tire out.

Several times during the fall and winter seasons, Jim would help chop firewood for those in the fellowship who had fireplaces. He really enjoyed being outside and took every opportunity to help someone.

Jim helped people who were not members of the

fellowship too. He was willing to help anyone. Whether it was a friend, neighbor, relative or someone on the street with car trouble, it made no difference to him. All he wanted to do was help whenever and wherever he could.

Although Jim didn't realize it for a long time, he was functioning in the ministry of helps and loving every minute of it.

MINISTRY OF HELPS

Scripture reading: Galatians 6:10

We are to look for opportunities to do good unto all men, especially to our brothers and sisters in Christ. The ministry of helps means doing good to our fellow-man.

This can be done in many different ways. Cooking meals for those who are sick, writing letters to those on the mission field, making clothes for those in need, helping fix a brother's car, or any number of other things. These we do in the name of Jesus, and He should get the glory and praise.

In Matthew 25:34-40, Jesus tells us that if we are kind to anyone, it is the same as being kind to Him. He mentions feeding the hungry, giving water to the thirsty, welcoming strangers, clothing the naked, and visiting the sick and imprisoned. These are only a few of the things we can do to help others.

We all should function in this ministry. This is not something that only one or two people from a church should do. Whenever we see a need either inside our church body or in the world outside, we should operate in the ministry of helps.

Questions:
1. What was Jim's special calling?
2. Do you know anyone like Jim?
3. Can you think of some way in which you can help someone?
4. Does a church need more than one helper?

Prayer:
Dear Lord, please use us in the ministry of helps. We all can do something to help another. Show us our part in this ministry in our church. In Jesus' name, amen.

27
Let's Have a Walk-a-Thon

"Hey, Peggy, wouldn't it be fun to have a walk-a-thon to support some missionary this summer?" Kathy asked.

"Yeah, that sounds like fun. Let's do it," Peggy agreed.

"We could get people to sponsor us for so much each mile and then we could collect after we walked. If we walk at least ten miles we could earn a lot of money," Kathy continued.

"Maybe we could get the whole church to help out," Peggy said. "If some of the mothers would bake cookies and make Kool-Aid for stops along the way, it would make our walk a little easier."

"And if the men would map out the route and walk along with us in case we had any trouble," Kathy said, "this could be a real fun project."

About that time dad pulled up in the driveway. "Just what are you two so excited about?" he asked.

The girls told dad all about their big plans to have a church walk-a-thon and of how great it would be to work together to support a missionary.

"That sounds like a great idea," dad agreed.

"Good!" said Peggy. "Now let's start calling all the kids and ask them if they want to help. Kathy, you call some of the mothers about the cookies."

"Wait a minute, girls," dad said. "Aren't you forgetting something very important?"

"What?" Kathy asked. "All we have to do is spread the word around and we can get this thing going real easy."

"But, Kathy, who told you it was okay to start a big project like this? Have you talked to any of the elders about it? Have you called the pastor yet?" dad questioned.

"Why do we have to go to all that trouble? We can organize this ourselves," Peggy argued. "They can help if they want to, but they don't have to do all the work."

"That isn't the point, girls. The point is that you don't have the authority to plan something that will involve the whole church," Dad insisted. "Besides, this will also reflect on the church throughout the whole community, so we must be careful to go about it in the right way. Now how about calling Pastor Long first and telling him your idea?"

Peggy and Kathy looked at each other and then back to dad. "Oh, okay," they agreed. "I guess it would be better to do it that way."

So the girls set up a meeting with Pastor Long and the elders of the church and explained their idea to them. Everyone agreed it was a good idea.

Next the girls met with Mr. Peterson, one of the deacons, and finished planning the details of the big event. They mapped out their route, made a list of volunteers to chaperone, and distributed the cookie and Kool-Aid responsibilities. Everything was well organized and a date was set.

Kathy and Peggy still played a big part in the walk-a-thon, but the approval had to come from the leaders of the church. The girls needed to learn that not everyone can make plans that affect the whole church. If each person planned their own activities without the approval of the governing leaders, what a mess we would have.

Soon people would have several things planned for

the same day, the mothers might be expected to bake cookies for five activities in the same week, or two people may invite guest speakers for the same weekend. This would make church life impossible and it would be a bad witness to the community.

This is why the ministry of governments is so important to a church. If it is functioning properly, everything will be well organized and in right order.

MINISTRY OF GOVERNMENTS

Scripture reading: Titus 1:5

The ministry of governments is the ruling authority in the church. This usually consists of the elders, deacons, and pastor of any group of believers.

The elders oversee the spiritual operations of the church. The deacons oversee the physical aspects, and the pastor is to guide in both areas.

The purpose of government in the church is to organize activities and take care of the spiritual growth of individual members. The members of the government are responsible for organizing meetings, getting guest speakers, keeping the teaching program moving, and many other things within the group.

Things like church building projects, outreach of the church in the community (nursing home services and jail programs), and organizing church functions would also be a part of this ministry.

Questions:
1. Was the girls' idea a good one?
2. Where did the problem start for Kathy and Peggy?
3. Have you ever tried to plan something without asking the leaders first?
4. Do you have elders in your church?

Prayer:
Heavenly Father, help us to respect those in authority over us. Show us how to function under their authority so that your name will be glorified. In Jesus' name, amen.

28
I Just Don't Understand

It was a lovely Sunday morning and everyone was enjoying the church service. Jonathan and Jodi sat in the front row singing and playing their tambourines.

After a beautiful time of song and praise, the building grew very still. Then Mr. Chase began speaking in an unknown tongue. Everyone sat quietly while he spoke.

Then there was another long silence, but no one brought an interpretation. After waiting several minutes, the pastor began to preach.

Jodi punched Jonathan in the side. "What was all that jabbering about? Did you know what he was saying?" she asked.

"Beats me," Jonathan said. "I sure don't know what Mr. Chase was trying to tell us. Let's ask Pastor Holmer after church."

"Okay," Jodi agreed.

After church the children asked their pastor what had happened during the service.

"Well, the Lord had something He wanted to tell us this morning," the pastor began. "Mr. Chase was obedient in bringing the message in tongues, but whoever had the interpretation, didn't obey. As a result, everyone was left wondering what God's message was. The tongues alone benefited no one. If someone would have interpreted the message, the whole body would have understood and received a blessing from it."

With this illustration, we can see that the ministry of tongues should not be used without an interpretation.

MINISTRY OF TONGUES

Scripture reading: 1 Corinthians 14:5

We must first understand that the ministry of

tongues is not the same as the gift of tongues. But there can be no ministry without the gift. The use of tongues within the church body is of value only as there is also an interpretation.

Tongues is a message from God to the church. It is a word of encouragement, instruction or correction. These messages are usually meant to build up or edify the church body.

The ministry of tongues in the church does not edify the people unless they understand what is said. That is why Paul said it would profit a church nothing if he spoke in tongues, unless the Lord also gave him the revelation of the tongue (1 Cor. 14:6).

Questions:
1. Was Mr. Chase wrong for bringing the message in tongues?
2. Did the church understand his words?
3. What other gift was needed to help them understand?
4. Has this ever happened in your church?

Prayer:
Dear Lord, help us to be obedient when you give us a message for the church, whether it be in tongues or in our native language. Show us how this ministry works in our own church. In Jesus' name, amen.

29
Now I Understand

One evening at church, after a time of song and praise, the congregation grew very quiet. Then Mr. Peterson began speaking in an unknown tongue. Everyone sat quietly while he spoke.

This was followed by a period of silence. Then Mrs. Kridley began to speak in English. The Holy Spirit spoke words of love and comfort to the people through her. He told of His great pleasure in their praises and of His desire to bless them. He told them of their need to seek Him daily in their prayer chambers and of the miracles He would do in their midst if they would be obedient.

Jason poked Steve on the arm. "Isn't that neat?" he asked. "God really must love us to take time to speak to us in church."

"Yeah, I sure am glad Mrs. Kridley told us what all those funny words meant," Steve said.

All the people who heard these words were wonderfully blessed. They were excited about what God had promised to do in their church if they would follow His instruction. Everyone left church that evening feeling happy and secure in God's love and looking forward to seeing His word fulfilled.

Now we can see the difference that is made when these two ministries work together. Tongues cannot operate alone, neither can the gift of interpretation. These ministries must work together or not at all.

MINISTRY OF INTERPRETATION

Scripture reading: 1 Corinthians 14:13-14

We learned in the last lesson that this ministry works together with that of tongues. If there is no message in tongues, there would be no need for an interpretation.

Paul tells us that if you bring a message in tongues and no one else brings the interpretation, you should ask God to give you the revelation of that message. Otherwise the body will not know what God is speaking to them.

It is not always necessary that the same person brings both the tongues and the interpretation. Very often one person will bring the tongue and another the interpretation. God operates in both ways, and we must be careful not to limit God and try to fit Him into our understanding.

Questions:
1. Did Steve and Jason understand Mr. Peterson's message?
2. Did they understand what Mrs. Kridley said?
3. What did God tell the church through this message?
4. How did the people feel after they heard it?

Prayer:
Dear Lord, teach us to know your voice and to obey your call. Let us understand all your ministries in and through the church. Help us to find our place in your body and let us give all the glory to you. In Jesus' name, amen.

PART FIVE

Walking With My Friend

30
Let's Pray About It

Kevin just didn't know what to do. He had never had a problem like this before. He had already asked his mother and his dad and his teacher what to do, but no one would tell him what he should do.

You see, Kevin had a chance to go to Texas for two weeks with his friend, Jerry. It sounded like real fun—riding horses, hunting cactus, seeing a real rodeo and many more exciting things.

The problem came when he realized his Aunt

Hattie was going to be visiting from New York during the same two weeks. Kevin hadn't seen his aunt for three years and he really wanted to spend some time with her, but he also wanted to go to Texas.

"Mom, you just have to help me make up my mind," Kevin said. "I have to let Jerry know by tomorrow."

"Well, Kevin, maybe you should pray about it and find out what the Lord wants you to do. We should ask God about everything we do, to make sure we are doing the right thing," mother answered.

"I guess you're right, mom, but how will I know what the Lord wants me to do?"

"You'll know, Kevin. You will feel a tug on your heart in the direction God wants you to go."

So Kevin went to his bedroom and thought about his problem some more. He tried to think of what Jesus would do in the same situation. Aunt Hattie was pretty old and she might not be able to make the trip again, but it would be such great fun to see a real cowboy.

"Oh, Lord, what should I do?" Kevin cried.

Before long Kevin came walking out of the bedroom with a big smile on his face. "Well, mom, I've made up my mind," Kevin began. "I'm going to stay here and visit with Aunt Hattie. I think she needs me more than I need to see those cowboys.

Besides there is always next year to go to Texas. Jerry goes to see his grandparents every summer."

Mother gave Kevin a big hug. "I'm so glad you decided that all by yourself. Dad and I wanted you to stay, but we felt you had to make the decision."

"Thanks, mom, but I didn't exactly decide by myself; God helped me to make the right decision. I sure am glad I prayed about it."

PRAYER

Scripture reading: 1 Thessalonians 5:17

We are to pray without ceasing. That means we are to pray without stopping. Of course, that doesn't mean God expects us to spend all day on our knees. Praying is just talking to God. We can talk to God when we are walking down the street, drying the dishes, or taking a bath. God just wants us to be willing and able to talk to Him whenever and wherever we are.

Christians need to pray about all things. We should learn to ask God about even the small things in our lives. Many people only talk to God when they have a big problem, but He wants us to talk to Him even when we don't have any problems.

We shouldn't just ask God for things either. God wants us to praise Him for what He has already done for us, and just to talk to Him as a friend. Of course, God wants to help us when we do have a problem so we should not be afraid to ask for His guidance and help.

God loves us very much and He wants His children to spend time with Him every day.

Questions:
1. Why did Kevin want to go to Texas?
2. Why was it so important for him to see Aunt Hattie?
3. Do you think Kevin made the right decision?
4. Do you pray about the things you do each day?

Prayer:
Dear Lord, teach us how to talk to you. Help us to pray always, so we can do what pleases you each day. Show us your love and let us know that you are truly our best friend. Amen.

31
Does It Really Say That?

When it finally stopped raining, Rick went outside to see what he could find to do. It was too wet to play ball and he was tired of riding his bike, so he decided to just take a walk to see if he could find something of interest.

As he rounded the corner, he looked over at Mr. Karber's front yard. It had just been planted in grass and now was a big area of gooey mud. Rick glanced both ways to see if anyone was watching. "This is going to be a riot," he thought as he slipped off his shoes.

Before long he was wading through the fresh grass seed, leaving only a sticky mess for a path. Rick was so fascinated by the cool mud squishing through his toes that he nearly fainted when he heard his sister's voice.

"What on earth are you doing? Mr. Karber will sure be mad when he sees this," Jenny said. "You better get out of there before he gets home and catches you."

"Oh, okay, you spoiled all the fun anyway," Rick growled. "You always have to worry about what the other guy thinks. You're such a fuddy-duddy."

With that, Rick stormed down the street toward home.

After Rick cleaned up a little, he went into the TV room. There he found Jenny reading her Bible. "Why are you always reading that thing?" he asked. "Is it really that interesting?"

"Yes, Rick, it is; and if you would read it more often, you would know just how wrong you were today," Jenny answered.

"You mean when I waded in Mr. Karber's yard? How could there be anything in the Bible about that?" Rick questioned.

"What about the Golden Rule?" Jenny asked. "Do unto others as you would have them do unto you.

Would you want someone to ruin a project you had just finished?"

"Well, of course not, but the Golden Rule isn't in the Bible. Someone just made that up because it sounded nice," Rick said.

"In Luke 6:31 it says, 'And as ye would that men should do to you, do ye also to them likewise.' " Jenny said, "That's the same thing; the words are just a little different."

"Hey, you're right! Let me see that," Rick said as he took the Bible from Jenny. "What else does it say in here?"

"The Bible tells us many things to help us live in a way that pleases God," Jenny continued. "But if you don't read the Bible, you'll never know what it says. That's why we should study God's Word every day. Then we'll know what is right and wrong for us to do."

"I sure am glad you showed me that Scripture. I knew I shouldn't mess up the grass seed, but I sure didn't know the Bible had anything to say about it."

Rick learned two very important things that afternoon. One, that if he had studied the Bible like he should, he would have known what was in it; and the other that when we do something wrong, we have to make it right again.

The next week Rick leveled off Mr. Karber's front yard and planted new grass seed. He also told Mr.

Karber how sorry he was for being so thoughtless and destructive.

BIBLE STUDY

Scripture reading: Psalm 119:11

This Scripture says that if we hide God's words in our hearts, we will not sin against Him. If we study the Bible, which is God's Word, we will know what things are good for us and what things are bad.

The Bible tells us everything we need to know about how to please God. It shows us how to find Jesus as our Savior, it explains about the Holy Spirit, and it tells us how to live a happy life.

The Bible tells us many wonderful stories of God's love. It tells about the miracles the Father and Jesus did. It teaches about healing, faith, love and so much more, but we will never know what the Bible says if we don't read and study it. That is why we should have time to read and pray every day, so we can hide these things in our hearts.

Questions:
1. Why did Rick run through the mud?
2. Who wrote the Golden Rule?

3. How did Jenny know what was in the Bible?
4. How can you know what is in God's Word?

Prayer:
Dear Lord, show us how important it is that we study your Word. Teach us to love the Bible. Help us to understand what we read and study and show us how to apply it to our lives. In Jesus' name, amen.

32
A Friend Named Jesus

Cindy just loved to go to Sunday school and church with her parents. She learned so many wonderful things about God the Father, Jesus and the Holy Spirit. She had invited Jesus into her heart a long time ago and how she loved to hear stories about Him.

One afternoon Cindy went over to visit her friend, Vicki. Vicki was playing with her dolls when Cindy came up the porch steps. "Hi! What are you up to?"

Cindy asked. "Can I play dolls with you?"

"Sure, you take this one and I will play with the one with the brown hair," Vicki said, handing Cindy the blonde doll.

As the girls played that afternoon, they talked about many things. Vicki wasn't a very happy little girl, but Cindy just couldn't find out why. She knew Vicki didn't see her dad much because he was a truck driver. They didn't have a lot of money, but that just didn't seem to be the reason either.

Finally Cindy just couldn't take it any more. "Vicki, why are you so unhappy?" she asked.

"I'm not really unhappy, I just feel so alone sometimes. When dad's driving the truck and mom is busy with the baby, I just don't have anyone to talk to. You come over once in a while, but I still have a lot of time to spend all alone."

"I guess I never thought about being alone," Cindy said. "My mom always has time to talk and my dad is home every night. And we can't forget my three brothers. I always have someone to talk to."

"Yeah, but at our house it is just me and the baby. Mom's always either busy with her or she is sewing or cleaning," Vicki continued. "I just wish I had a friend I could talk to anytime and someone who would understand how I feel."

"I have a friend like that," Cindy said. "He is always ready to listen to me and He always understands."

"Really? Who is it?" Vicki asked.

"His name is Jesus. He is God's Son and He loves everyone very much," Cindy said. "You could come to Sunday school with me if you want to learn more about Him. I'm sure you would like to hear all the stories of the wonderful things Jesus does for His friends."

"I sure would like to know this Jesus. He sounds like just what I need to make my life happy like yours," Vicki said. "I'll ask mom if I can go."

Vicki went to Sunday school with Cindy and she found out just what a special friend Jesus can be. Because Cindy was willing to share her love for Jesus, Vicki found the way to real happiness.

WITNESSING

Scripture reading: Mark 5:19

The Bible tells us we should speak to others about the great things the Lord has done for us. When we have Jesus in our hearts, we should be excited about sharing Him with our friends. Everyone needs a good friend to talk to—someone to whom he can tell secret thoughts. Jesus can be that friend.

Once we have Jesus as our friend, we need to talk to others about Him, so they can find this wonderful friend also. This is called "witnessing." That just means telling others about what the Lord has done for you. When God heals you, you should be sure to give Him the praise and tell someone you have been healed. When the Lord answers a special prayer for you, you should go right out and tell someone that God has been good to you.

This is how others will learn that God is good and loving and then they will want to know more about Him and His Son, Jesus.

Questions:
1. Why was Vicki so unhappy?
2. What did Cindy tell her to make her feel better?
3. Who was Vicki's new friend?
4. Do you know someone who needs a friend?

Prayer:
Dear Lord, help us to be bold in telling others about you. Show us who we should talk to and give us just the right words to say. Let us always be willing to share our friend, Jesus, with others. In His name, amen.

33
Where Have You Been?

"Hey, Larry! Let's play a little football," Doug called from across the street.

"Sure, come on over. I'll go get the ball."

By the time Doug reached the back steps, Larry was coming out of the garage with the ball under his arm. "Catch this pass," he yelled, as he hurled the ball at Doug.

"What have you been doing all summer?" Doug asked. "I haven't seen you much."

"Oh, we've been around most of the time. We did go to Michigan for two weeks in July, but otherwise we've been home."

"Really, I thought you had gone away for the whole summer," Doug said.

"Where did you get an idea like that?" Larry asked.

The boys put the ball down and planted themselves under a big tree.

"Well," Doug began, "you haven't been to church or Sunday school for at least two months, so I thought you were out of town."

"No, I just decided I didn't need to spend that much time in church," Larry said. "I can be just as good a Christian at home. I still read the Bible and pray every day."

"But don't you miss seeing the other kids at church?" Doug asked.

"Yeah, but I have other friends. I went to the stock car races the other night with Duke Snyder and we had a great time. He even showed me how to jump the fence so I didn't have to pay to get in."

"I don't think that kind of friend is going to bring you closer to Jesus," Doug said. "That guy gets in a lot of trouble.

"Hey, we are having a church hayride next weekend; do you think you can come?" Doug asked. "We are going to have a wiener roast afterwards at the Collins' farm. It is going to be a lot of fun."

"Okay, I guess I could come," Larry said.

When Larry saw how much fun he had with the kids from the church, he decided to start going again. He had forgotten how much he liked Sunday school and he really did feel better when he was with other kids who loved Jesus like he did.

Larry found out he needed to stay in fellowship with others who loved the Lord. Larry could have remained a Christian even if he didn't go to church, but it is best to be with people who share our love for the Lord. In that way we can help and encourage them and they can do the same for us.

FELLOWSHIP

Scripture reading: Hebrews 10:25

God's Word tells us that we should meet together with other Christians. This alone is enough reason for doing it. If God says it, we don't need any other reason.

By having fellowship with others who love the Lord, we can encourage them to keep trusting in God, we can pray for them, and we can tell them of the good things God is doing in our lives. If we never see another Christian, how can we know if they have any prayer needs, or how will we know if they have a problem in understanding a certain Scripture. There are many good things that come from Christians meeting together.

When you look at all the trouble in the newspapers and when you see all the bad things on television, it is wonderful to know you have friends who love Jesus and are praying for you.

Having fellowship with other Christians helps us to grow together in the Lord. It also helps us to love God and each other more. That is the way God wants His people to be.

Questions:
1. Why did Doug think Larry had been gone all summer?
2. Did Duke help Larry to live for Jesus?
3. What is fellowship?
4. Why should we have fellowship with other Christians?

Prayer:
Dear Lord, show us just how important it is to stay in fellowship with other Christians. Help us to grow more like you every day and let us help our friends to know more about you. Bring us into fellowship with you and with others who love you. In Jesus' name, amen.

34
Oops! I Forgot!

It was a hot morning and Janie and Scot were anxious to get to the swimming pool and cool off.

"Mom, can we go swimming today?" Scot asked. "It sure is hot enough."

"I think it'll be okay for you to go swimming this afternoon, but you have work to do this morning," mother said.

"What work?" Janie grumbled. "I get so tired of doing jobs around here."

"Well, your dad and I get tired, too, but if the work is there, someone has to do it," mother replied.

Mother handed them a list of things to do before they could go swimming: take out the trash, feed the dog, make their beds, and put the bikes and toys away in the garage. Janie and Scot groaned as they left the kitchen to start their chores.

Before long it was lunch time and Mother called Janie and Scot in to eat. "Did you get all the chores done?" she asked.

"Sure, mom, what do you think we've been doing all morning?" Scot answered. "Now can we go swimming right after lunch?"

"I guess so, if you are sure you did all I asked."

"Mother, we did!" Janie insisted.

Right after lunch Janie and Scot grabbed their suits and towels and headed for the pool. On the way down the driveway Janie stopped short. "Look, Scot, we forgot to put your new bike in the garage."

"That's okay, we'll do it when we get home," Scot said.

"But, Scot, we told mom that we did all the jobs she gave us. She'll be mad when she sees that bike there," Janie said.

"Janie, we'll be back before she notices it. Now stop worrying about it."

So Janie and Scot spent the afternoon playing at the park and swimming pool. In fact, they stayed even longer than they had planned. When they finally got home, they saw their dad's car in the driveway.

"Oh boy, are we in trouble!" Janie said.

"Maybe not," Scot said. "Just stay cool until we get the bike put away."

As they walked around the car, Scot nearly choked. There in front of him he saw a twisted heap of metal and tires that used to be his bike.

"Pretty, isn't it?" dad said from the doorway. "I understand your bike should have been put away before you went swimming. Right?"

"Yes, sir. It should have been in the garage," Scot answered.

"Well, it isn't going to be a very fun summer without a bike, but I don't intend to buy a new one," dad said. "If you two had obeyed your mother, this would never have happened!"

"But, dad, what about my paper route? I need a bike for that," Scot argued.

"I guess you'll just have to walk. That will give you lots of time to think about the importance of obeying your parents," dad replied.

"You children know how much we have stressed not leaving things in the driveway," mother said. "It is impossible to see past that bush over there, so when something is in the driveway, it just gets hit."

"I really am sorry about your bike, Scot," dad

began. "But you still deserve some punishment for your disobedience, and you too, Janie. You both are old enough to understand what it means to obey and you purposefully chose not to put the bike away."

"But, dad, I've already lost my bike," Scot argued. "Isn't that enough?"

"I think if you both stay home from the pool for a week, you might take our words a little more seriously," mom and dad agreed.

Janie and Scot looked at each other in dismay, but deep down they knew their parents were right.

OBEDIENCE

Scripture reading: Ephesians 6:1

It is very important that we learn to obey our parents in all they say because that is what God tells us to do. Parents love their children and desire to do what is best for them.

Sometimes we think mom and dad aren't being fair about things, but we should still listen to what they say and be careful to obey them.

In learning to obey our earthly parents, we will be better able to obey our heavenly Father when He tells us to do something.

If your parents love the Lord, you can be sure they are trying to teach you the best things they know. Their teaching will help you grow up into a responsible and respectable adult.

Questions:
1. What is disobedience?
2. What did Janie and Scot do that was wrong?
3. Did they know that they would get in trouble?
4. Were their parents being mean by punishing them?

Prayer:
Dear Lord, show us why it is important to obey our parents. Help us to be willing to learn obedience. Teach us also to obey your voice, so we can do your will in our lives. In Jesus' name, amen.

35
I'm Gonna Punch You!

It was late afternoon and the kids had just gotten home from school. Mother was in the kitchen starting supper. Suddenly there was such a racket from the other room.

"I did, too!" Phil shouted.

"You did not!" Carol argued.

"I'll prove it to you," Phil continued, "right after I punch you in the nose!"

"Mom! Phil is going to hit me!" Carol yelled.

By this time mother was standing in the doorway looking very unhappy. "What are you two fighting about this time?" she asked.

"Carol said I didn't get an A on my spelling test and I did," Phil said, pointing to his paper. "See, right there it is. She is so dumb; why did I have to get her for a sister?"

"That's enough from both of you," mother said. "All you two do is fight and argue. And most of the time it is over nothing at all. Now go do your homework."

Mother went back to the kitchen and started peeling the potatoes. Before long she could hear Phil and Carol at it again.

"You better give that back or I'll sock you a good one," Carol said. "That's my ruler and you can't use it."

"Do you think you're big enough to take it from me?" Phil laughed. "Let's see you try."

Carol stood on her tiptoes and tried to reach the ruler. She just wasn't tall enough to get it out of Phil's hands when he raised them over his head. She pulled back her fist and gave him a punch.

"Oof! Mom, she hit me in the stomach," Phil moaned. "Oh, I think I'm going to be sick."

"Good! Now give me back my ruler," Carol said as she grabbed it from his hands.

"Okay, you guys," mother began. "Sit down, both

of you. Now just what is the problem here?"

"He took my ruler, and I got it back. It's just that simple," Carol said.

"Yeah, but she hit me too," Phil groaned, holding his stomach.

"I think you both need to learn to share things," mother said. "You know the Lord isn't happy when He hears you arguing all the time. Couldn't you just take turns with the ruler?"

Phil and Carol just looked at each other. They hadn't even thought about how Jesus would feel when they didn't get along.

"I really wish you children would pray and ask the Lord to help you get along better," mother continued. "It isn't very pleasant around here with you two yelling and punching each other."

"I guess you're right, mom," Phil said. "We don't try very hard."

"I didn't even know the Lord could help us get along better," Carol said, "or I would have asked Him a long time ago."

With both Phil and Carol trying harder to get along, things began to improve in their home. Whenever they started to get angry, they asked Jesus to help them agree. Of course, they still had some disagreements, but now they had the Lord to help them straighten things out. As a result, they had fewer arguments and almost no punching. The Lord helped them to become a true Christian brother and sister.

KEEPING PEACE

Scripture reading: Philippians 2:14

This Scripture tells us that we should do all things without complaining or arguing. That's a hard rule to follow. If I tried to tell you it was easy, I wouldn't be telling the truth. Some of God's rules are hard, but we still need to obey them.

If we can just learn to get things in the right order, it will be much easier for us to obey. To have JOY we need to put *J*esus first, *O*thers next, and *Y*ourself last. That's easy to remember because when you put the first letters of these words together they spell JOY. That is the only way to keep the peace and joy of the Lord in our hearts.

If we keep things in this order, I doubt if we will get into many arguments. There is no need for fighting when you put the other person's thoughts and feelings first.

Questions:
1. Why did Carol punch Phil?

2. Was she right in doing it?
3. Have you ever had a fight with someone?
4. Is that the best way to solve a problem?

Prayer:
Dear Lord, show us how to get along with other people. Teach us to keep you first, others second and ourselves last so we can have your joy in our lives. In Jesus' name, amen.

36
Jack Did It

The bright sun shone through the kitchen window as Tommy sat finishing his breakfast. With his mouth still full of cereal, he grabbed his ball glove and ran out to meet Jack.

As Tommy walked down the street to the vacant lot on the corner, he met his neighbor, Mr. Dunn. "Good morning, Tommy. Are you going to play catch again this morning?"

"Yes, Mr. Dunn. Jack is going to meet me on the

corner in a few minutes."

"Well, you boys have a good time, but be careful. I just put a new pane in my picture window and you know that it faces the lot where you always play."

"Oh, sure, Mr. Dunn. We'll be very careful."

Just then Jack came running across the lot with his ball and glove in hand. "Sorry I'm late. I had to take out the trash before I came."

"That's all right. You just missed a lecture from dear old Mr. Dunn."

"Really?" questioned Jack. "What did he say?"

"Oh, I guess he thinks we can't catch and that we'll break his new window," answered Tommy.

"Well, let's play some catch before I have to go for my piano lesson," Jack said.

Everything went fine for a few minutes. Then Tommy pulled back his arm and threw the ball just as hard as he could. Jack jumped to try to catch it, but he just couldn't reach it. Crash!

"Oh, no!" yelled Jack. "Now we did it; we really did it this time! We broke that new window!"

Tommy's eyes nearly popped out of his head. "Now what do we do? I guess we'll have to wait until Mr. Dunn gets home and explain it to him."

"But, Tommy, I can't wait here. It's time for my lesson."

"You go ahead, Jack. I'll tell him and call you later to let you know what he wants to do."

After Jack left, Tommy started thinking about the cost of that big window pane. He had been saving his money to buy a new bike for summer vacation. If he had to pay for half of that window, he wouldn't have enough money left to buy a bike for several weeks. If there was just some way to get out of paying for his share. Well, maybe there was.

Tommy's thoughts were interrupted by the sound of someone running up the sidewalk. "What did I tell you boys about that window?" yelled Mr. Dunn. "I just can't believe it. I just warned you, not even an hour ago—and where did that Jack go?"

Tommy was scared stiff, but he had to say something. "Well, uh, Mr. Dunn, Jack went home. He threw the ball at your shrubs and when it hit the window instead, he ran home. I guess he was plenty scared."

"Well, he should be! Just wait 'til I get my hands on him." With that, Mr. Dunn stormed down the street to Jack's house.

Tommy was safely home by the time Mr. Dunn reached Jack's front door. He stomped up the steps and pounded hard on the door. Jack wasn't surprised to see him, but he was surprised to hear the story Tommy had told.

After Mr. Dunn had finished telling Tommy's version of what had happened, Jack told him what had really taken place.

"Well, I'm really sorry this happened," Jack began, "but I do want to pay for my share of the new window. The only problem is that I don't have any money, and it wouldn't be fair to ask my parents to pay for something I broke. Do you think I could work out my share of the expense?"

"Sure, I think we could work something out like that. How about if you mow my lawn on Saturday and then next week after school you can help me plow and plant my garden?"

"That sounds just great, Mr. Dunn, and I really am sorry about this whole mess."

Mr. Dunn smiled as he opened the door to leave. "I sure am glad we had this talk, but I'm not so sure that Tommy will be. I think I'd better go talk to him too. Bye."

Tommy had been thinking about all the things he had said and of how wrong he had been to have blamed Jack for the broken window. He was nearly in tears when he saw Mr. Dunn through the screen door. "I know what you came for, Mr. Dunn, and I'm so ashamed of the way I lied to you. I hope you will forgive me for being such a dope. I knew you would find out the truth from Jack. He wouldn't tell a lie to save his life."

"Jack knows it never pays to be dishonest because you always get caught sooner or later," Mr. Dunn began. "Besides, breaking a window isn't the end of the world."

Tommy handed Mr. Dunn his bank. "Here, you figure out what is my share and then you can bring back the rest. I may have to wait a little longer for that new bike, but at least I will still have a friend to ride with me."

TRUTHFULNESS

Scripture reading: Ephesians 4:25

The Bible tells us that we should speak the truth to all men. There is never a good reason for telling a lie and there is no such thing as a little white lie. Any lie is wrong and a sin in God's sight.

We should be very careful to always tell the whole truth, too.

When we stretch the truth to make a story sound more exciting, we are really telling a lie. When we only tell part of the truth to keep from getting into trouble, we are also telling a lie.

When we do something bad, it is better to tell the truth and take our punishment than it is to lie about it and then feel bad inside. It is the Holy Spirit that makes us feel bad when we do something wrong. When we feel that way in our hearts, it is because the

Lord wants us to tell Him the truth and say we are sorry, so He can forgive us.

Then we can be happy again and go on living for the Lord.

Questions:
1. Why did Tommy tell a lie?
2. Who really broke the window?
3. Have you ever told a lie?
4. Who makes us feel bad when we don't tell the truth?

Prayer:
Dear Lord, show us how important it is to always tell the whole truth. Help us to be completely honest no matter what, so we will please you. In Jesus' name, amen.

37
He Loves Me No Matter What!

Bobby woke up and looked out the window. It was a beautiful day outside and he should have been excited about going out to play, but he wasn't.

"Good morning, Bobby," his mother said.

"Yeah, I guess so."

"What do you mean, you *guess* so?" mother asked. "Are you still down in the dumps?"

She reached down and ruffled his hair. "You'll feel better after you have some breakfast."

Breakfast was good, but it still didn't help, so Bobby decided to go outside.

As Bobby stepped off the front porch, he noticed the neighbor kids playing across the street. They were laughing and singing and having a great time. Bobby decided to go behind the house and sit under the old apple tree. That was always a good place to go when he wanted to think.

Bobby tried very hard to think things out. Just what was he feeling? He didn't feel sick, but he didn't really feel all that well either. He didn't feel sad, but he sure wasn't happy. He didn't feel afraid of anything. He wasn't mad at anyone, so he didn't feel like fighting. But he wasn't glad about anything, so he didn't feel like laughing either. The only thing Bobby knew for sure was that he was very confused.

Bobby could hear his mother in the kitchen doing the breakfast dishes. When he turned around and looked in the window, he saw that his mother was crying.

"Oh, no," Bobby mumbled, "now look what I've done. I know mom is crying because of me."

Bobby got up and ran around to the front of the house. He was very quiet so mother wouldn't hear him. He tiptoed upstairs and got his suitcase from under his bed and quickly packed his things. As he looked around the room to see what else he needed, he noticed the picture of Jesus on his dresser. He took it down and safely tucked it between his pajamas. Then Bobby went to his desk and scribbled down this note:

Dear mom and dad,
When I saw mom crying this morning, I knew I had been trouble for you. I love you and I don't want to hurt you. I know I have been bad to you, but I don't think anyone understands me, and I don't understand you either. I know you can't love me when I am this way, so I am leaving.
         Bobby
P.S. I'll always love you, no matter what.

Bobby tiptoed back down the stairs and pinned the note to the front screen door where his dad would be sure to find it when he came home for lunch.

Then Bobby just started walking. He didn't really know where he wanted to go, so he just kept going. Soon he got tired and hungry. He only had $2.37 so he went into a little diner on the corner. He peeked at the menu before he sat down.

When the waitress came she asked, "What will it be today, kiddo?"

"Just a bowl of chili and a glass of milk. I'm not very hungry today." Bobby really was very hungry, but he had to make his money last as long as he could.

Meanwhile, his dad had found the note.

"Well, he couldn't have gotten very far," dad said as he tried to comfort mom. "I guess we had better call the police and let them handle the search. That way we can wait here in case he comes home on his own." Mother nodded in agreement.

Bobby finished his chili and curled up in the booth in the diner and fell asleep. He didn't know what his parents had done and since he was sleeping, Bobby didn't have a chance to make a getaway.

The next thing he knew someone was tugging on his shirt sleeve. "Hey, little fella, wake up."

Much to Bobby's surprise it was a policeman. He seemed at least seven feet tall and he had a big gun on his hip. Bobby was scared to death.

"Wait!" Bobby pleaded, "I paid for the chili and I didn't do anything wrong. I—I— I'm sorry for falling asleep, but—"

The policeman gently put his hand over Bobby's mouth. "Slow down, fella. I'm not going to arrest you, but I do know someone who would like to talk to you."

"Oh, okay. I'll go with you. Just, just don't put me in jail."

Bobby was so scared he would have agreed to anything just to keep that policeman smiling.

When the police cruiser pulled up in front of Bobby's house, his parents came running across the lawn. Once Bobby was safely home, the policeman smiled, waved, and went on his way.

Bobby looked at his dad's face and wondered what would happen next.

"Son, I just don't know what to do with you," he began. Then he stopped. In the shuffle, Bobby's suitcase had fallen and its contents scattered on the lawn. They all saw the picture of Jesus escape from its place of safety.

"Why did you take this picture with you, Bobby?" dad asked.

"Because I knew that whatever I did, or whatever I felt, or even however dumb I was acting, Jesus would always love me and be my friend."

Dad picked up the picture and took Bobby in his arms. "Remember, Bobby, we will always love you too—no matter what."

ASSURANCE

Scripture reading: Deuteronomy 31:6

God's Word tells us that we never need to feel alone because He is always with us. We never have to be afraid; He will not forsake us. Through all our troubles and confusion, the Lord will comfort and guide us.

Even when we act like we don't love the Lord, He

still cares for us. No matter what we do or say, the Holy Spirit keeps tugging at our hearts.

Jesus is a wonderful friend. He always understands how we feel and never gets angry with us. Sometimes we hurt Him by our unbelief or by being disobedient, but He still loves us.

People get mad and might even stop wanting to be our friend, but Jesus is always there to help us. He is always willing to listen to our problems and ready to forgive us when we do wrong.

It is wonderful to know we can count on our friend Jesus in every situation and He will never fail.

Questions:
1. Why did Bobby run away?
2. What was he feeling?
3. Why did he take the picture with him?
4. Did you ever feel like Bobby?

Prayer:
Dear Lord, remind us of your everlasting love. Show us just how much you care. Keep us in your hands and make us feel safe there. We want you to always be our friend. In Jesus' name, amen.

38
I Don't Need Your Help!

Laura sat looking out the window at the snow falling on the sidewalk. She had been thinking of all the things she wanted to do that day and how everyone was always trying to help her. Just because she was only six years old was no reason why she couldn't do some things for herself. After all, she had a right to do things her way once in a while.

"That's it," she said. "Today I won't let anyone help me do anything. I'll show them I can do things alone."

Just then Laura's mother came in. "Laura, do you want me to help you put on your boots so you can go out to play?"

"No, I do not, mother!" Laura shouted. "I can do it myself."

"Well, all right, but you needn't be so snappy about it."

"Well, you never let me do anything," Laura continued. "You and dad and Chad think you are the only ones who can do anything."

"Okay, Laura, you can do it yourself. I'm going next door for a cup of coffee. If you need me, just call."

"Don't worry, mom, I won't need you."

Laura put her boots on just fine and didn't have a bit of trouble. Then her older brother, Chad, came in. In his hands he carried two new pairs of ice skates. "Look what mom bought for us, Laura."

"Wow! Those are really neat, Chad. Let's go try them out on the pond. Wait 'til Nancy sees me sailing across the ice," Laura's voice chimed with excitement.

"But you don't even know how to skate," Chad said. "You'll probably fall and kill yourself. You'd better let me help, at least at first. After all, I have been skating for two years."

Laura was furious! She grabbed her shiny new

skates and ran out the door. Chad just stood there and watched her as she ran across the field toward the pond.

When Laura reached the pond, Nancy and Donnie were already on the ice. Of course, they were older and already knew how to skate. Laura sat on the log next to the campfire to put on her new skates.

Now she was ready to show everyone she could skate too, and she didn't need anyone to help her either. She stood up, wobbled a little and down she went.

About this time Chad had reached the pond and was watching Laura from behind a tree. "Ha, ha, ha," Chad laughed. "I thought you knew how to skate, Laura."

"Oh, you just shut up and leave me alone, Chad. Who asked you anyway?" Laura got up and tried again. This time she managed to wobble out onto the ice. Her form was far from graceful, but at least she was still on her feet.

Chad finished lacing his skates and glided across the ice to meet Donnie and Nancy. "Hi, guys. How's the ice?"

"Just great, Chad. Hey, watch this spin!"

"That was real neat, Donnie. When did you learn to do that?"

"Say, Chad, where is Laura?"

In the excitement of the new skates and the

spinning, everyone had forgotten about Laura. As they looked across the pond, they could see she was having a little trouble staying on her feet, but at least she was trying and she was doing it all by herself.

As Nancy practiced her figure eights and Chad and Donnie tried to out-spin each other, they were reminded of a very important fact they had failed to mention to Laura. "Oh, no!" Nancy exclaimed. "We forgot to warn Laura about the ice in the center of the pond. It isn't frozen solid yet and she shouldn't skate out there."

"That's right," said Chad, "especially not alone."

By the time the frightened trio reached Laura, she was well on her way to the center of the pond. "Hey, Laura!" Donnie called. "Don't go out there in the center. The ice isn't solid."

Laura turned and looked at them in disgust. "You just don't think I can skate that far. I know you guys. You just don't want me to have any fun. I'll show you I can skate and I can do it all by myself too."

"Laura, please don't go over there," Chad pleaded.

Laura had made up her mind that no one was going to stop her this time. Those "dumb kids" weren't going to make her feel silly again. Laura just knew the older kids were teasing about the ice not being safe. They just wanted her to ask for their help and she wasn't about to do that, no matter what.

If Laura had glided across the center ice with one

graceful sweep, perhaps all would have been well; but with her faltering and falling, it just wouldn't work.

She could now see that she was in trouble, but her pride wouldn't let her call for help. As the ice cracked under her skates, Laura tried harder to get away from the weak spot. In her efforts to escape, she fell through the ice and into the icy water.

"Help! Help!"

By the time Laura decided to call for help, Chad and Donnie had already started toward her. Nancy headed for the house to get help.

The water was so cold and besides that, Laura didn't know how to swim very well. She kept trying to hold onto the ice, but it just kept breaking and the hole was getting bigger and bigger.

Nancy came running across the ice with her dad and Laura's mom. They had a big rope which they threw to Laura.

"I can't reach it, mom," Laura cried, "and my hands are so cold I can't hold on to it anyway."

They pulled the rope back and made a loop on the end. This time they threw it and Laura grabbed it. "Put the loop around your waist so we can pull you out," called Donnie.

Laura felt as if she would soon be completely frozen, but she managed to get the loop over her head. Then they pulled her out of the water and across the ice to a solid spot. They wrapped her in a blanket and carried her home.

It really felt good to be in that warm house. After she had had a hot bath, Laura curled up in a blanket in front of the fireplace. "Boy, mom, I sure am glad that this time you guys didn't listen to me and try to let me do it all by myself. I guess I learned a lesson today. Sometimes it is smarter to let someone help."

"Well, Laura, no one can do everything by himself. We all need the help of our friends and family sometimes. The important thing is that you are safe now and that you know much we all love you."

"Yeah, mom, and I love you, too," Laura answered.

"And I even love you, Chad."

With that remark they all laughed and hugged each other. Laura had learned that it isn't always good to say, "I can do it myself."

RECEIVING MINISTRY

Scripture reading: 1 Peter 3:8

We all like to do some things for ourselves. The problem starts when we think no one but us can do a certain thing, or when we need help, but refuse to ask for it.

As God's children, we are part of a big family. The Lord wants us to be able to help each other and to trust our brothers and sisters for help with our problems.

We cannot live this life all alone. Sooner or later the Lord will put us in a position where we need some help. If He didn't, we might become proud and boastful and forget the Lord is in control.

As Christians we need to learn that every one of God's children has a place in His work. None of us can do everything well. We need each other to make the church complete.

God's church body is just like our human body in some ways. We need our eyes very much, but we also need our feet. Our hands are very important, but we would not be complete without our noses. Each part of our bodies is needed and each part of God's church body is needed.

Only when we each do our part and work together will the church function as the Lord wants it to. So remember that no matter how good a Christian you are, or how strong you think you are, you still need your brothers and sisters in Christ.

Questions:
1. Why did Laura skate off by herself?
2. Did someone try to help her?

3. Have you ever wanted to do something all by yourself?
4. Is it good to have people who will help us?

Prayer:
Dear Lord, make us willing to ask for help when we need it. Show us how to work together with our brothers and sisters so that your will can be done. In Jesus' name, amen.

39
Don't You Ever Get Tired?

"Hey, mom, what are we doing next Saturday?" Beth asked. "Judy wants me to go shopping with her."

"We have to clean the church, Beth, but I guess we can get along without your help this time."

"How come you always have to be the one to clean?" Beth continued. "There are lots of other people who could take a turn. It just isn't fair."

"I know it seems that way," mother said, "and we

do get tired of doing it, but we can't expect people to worship in a dirty building."

"Yeah, I guess so," Beth said as she ducked out the back door.

A few minutes later Beth came into the kitchen. "Now what are you doing?" she asked.

"I am baking cookies for the fellowship after church Sunday," mother answered. "I thought I would make two kinds so there will be plenty to go around."

"Is everyone else bringing some too?" Beth asked.

"Well, I think so, but someone always forgets. So, just to be safe, I'll bring some extra," mother said.

"Oh, mom, how can you keep up with all the stuff you do for the church?" Beth said rather disgustedly.

"It is important to understand that we do these things for the Lord, not for the church or for people," mother began. "It doesn't matter how many jobs we have, if we remember we're working for Jesus and not to please people. We'll always have enough strength to finish and will have the determination to do the job well."

"You make it sound so easy," Beth said. "I sure would get tired of that real quick. I have other things I like to do instead of working for church gatherings. You even teach Sunday school and the ladies' Bible study. I just don't know how you do it."

"I didn't say it was always easy," mother replied,

"but I know God will reward my faithfulness; besides, those other people miss a blessing by not getting involved in the less exciting church activities. If everyone did the nice jobs and left the common things undone, before long we would be in big trouble."

"Well, I guess you're right," Beth agreed, "but I sure hope everyone appreciates what you're doing."

"Even if they don't, it's okay," mother said, "because I know the Lord appreciates all that I do."

CHRISTIAN SERVICE

Scripture reading: Galatians 6:9

We should not grow weary of doing good things. In due season, or when the time is right, God will bless us and we'll reap the good things we have sown.

There are many things involved in running a church, business, or home that are not fun and games. It's hard work to keep things going smoothly. It isn't easy for your father to go to work every day, and then mow the grass and weed the garden when he gets home. It isn't easy for your mother to do the laundry, clean the house and cook every day. Your parents do this because they love you and want to do good things for you.

We should be the same way about helping others. Jesus was always willing to help someone in need. He even went without eating and sleeping sometimes just to help a friend. Since He is our perfect example, we should try to be as much like Him as possible.

It's nice to always get the fun jobs, like baking cookies or passing out the Sunday school treats, but it takes a special kind of person to enjoy emptying the trash.

Some of the most important jobs in God's kingdom are things no one ever sees. There isn't much excitement in mopping the floors of the church, but would you like to worship in a room that was all dusty and tracked with mud?

Teaching Sunday school seems like a lot of fun, but there are many hours of studying to get ready. And what about those lovely glue-together pictures and crafts you make? Did you ever think of how long it takes to cut out fifty snowflakes and all the other things that go into making your picture? Your teacher puts lot of work and love into each lesson she prepares.

The thing that makes it all worthwhile is knowing that we are working to please the Lord and not people. It doesn't matter if people ever notice what we have done, because God sees all things and He will reward us.

Questions:
1. Why didn't Beth's mother get tired of doing good things?
2. What was her secret?
3. Do you always want the nice jobs?
4. What other job could you do today?

Prayer:
Dear Lord, help us to be willing to do some things that aren't always fun. Show us how important the common jobs can be. Teach us what it means to "not grow weary in well doing." In Jesus' name, amen.

40
To Be a Winner

"Hey, mom! What's there to eat? I'm starved," Cory yelled as he ran in the front door. "That track practice is something else. Would you believe we had to run around the whole building twice and then up and down the bleachers?"

Mother smiled as she looked at her bedraggled son slouched across the chair. "You look bushed," she said. "I'll get you a sandwich and some milk to hold you until dinner."

"That sounds great," Cory said.

"How often do you have to practice like that, Cory?"

"Every night after school. Our first meet is next Friday, so we have to get in shape," Cory answered.

"That sounds like a lot of work. Are you sure you want to stay on the team?" mother asked.

"It is hard training, but it will all be worth it when we win that track meet for good old Ross High."

Cory did work very hard every day, not only with the team after school, but even doing exercises at home. He also had to watch what he ate so he didn't put on any weight before the meet. Sometimes his muscles hurt so bad that he had to rub the knots out of them, but he just kept right on practicing. Cory knew he couldn't win a race by just walking out in front of a cheering crowd and running. It took lots of hard work and pain to do the job right.

Soon the night of the first track meet arrived and the team was ready to run their best and fastest. Several strong young men entered the cross country event. Cory had also chosen this as one of his specialties. As the starting gun sounded, they all left the line in a flash.

The farther the boys got along the track, the more they slowed down or dropped out. Some of those who left the starting line the fastest were now dragging behind. Cory wasn't the first out of the starting gate, but he was one of the few who had been able to maintain a steady pace throughout the course.

With only a few yards to go to reach the finish line, Cory began to pick up speed. The other runners had already used most of their energy. Slowly but surely Cory worked his way to the lead position and held it. The crowd was cheering excitedly as Cory tore through the ribbon marking the finish.

"Cory, that was a great race!" the coach said. "That was real smart to save your burst of energy until the last minute."

"Thanks, coach," Cory puffed, "I only did what you taught us to do. Without all those practices, I would never have made it."

"Cory, we are so proud of you," mother said. "I am so glad you decided that all the work and pain were worth it."

"Son, you sure made me happy tonight," dad added. "I knew I raised a winner."

COMMITMENT

Scripture reading: 2 Timothy 4:7-8

The example of Cory and the track team is much like us in our Christian walk. This Scripture tells us that if we win the fight, finish the course and keep our faith, God will reward us.

Notice that the Bible does not say everyone who starts the race will get a prize. It doesn't matter who starts first, or even who keeps the best form, or who runs the fastest; it is the one who endures to the end. Every person who runs the full course with Jesus wins the crown of righteousness.

Many times we will come against problems during our walk with the Lord, just like a runner may trip over a stone during a race. The idea is to get back up and continue on whatever the cost.

Sometimes we get sore spiritual muscles and we really feel like giving up. That is when we need to rub on the oil of gladness and bandage ourselves with the love of Jesus. For every ache and pain along the way, God has just the right liniment in His Word. Our job is to find and apply it.

Just as there is much work and practice in the sport of track, there is much preparation and determination in the Christian walk. The main thing is to keep moving and never give up. We can draw strength from God's Word, the love of Jesus and the ministry of the Holy Spirit, so we have no excuse for not finishing the race. The Lord has given us all the provisions before we need them.

Questions:
1. Why do we need to practice our faith?

2. Did Cory win without a fight?
3. What do you think we mean by a "spiritual muscle"?
4. Are you going to finish the race?

Prayer:
Dear Lord, let us practice our faith daily. Show us how to be winners. Help us to endure until the day we see Jesus face to face. In His name, amen.

For free information on how to receive
the international magazine

LOGOS JOURNAL

also Book Catalog

Write: Information - LOGOS JOURNAL CATALOG
       Box 191
       Plainfield, NJ 07061